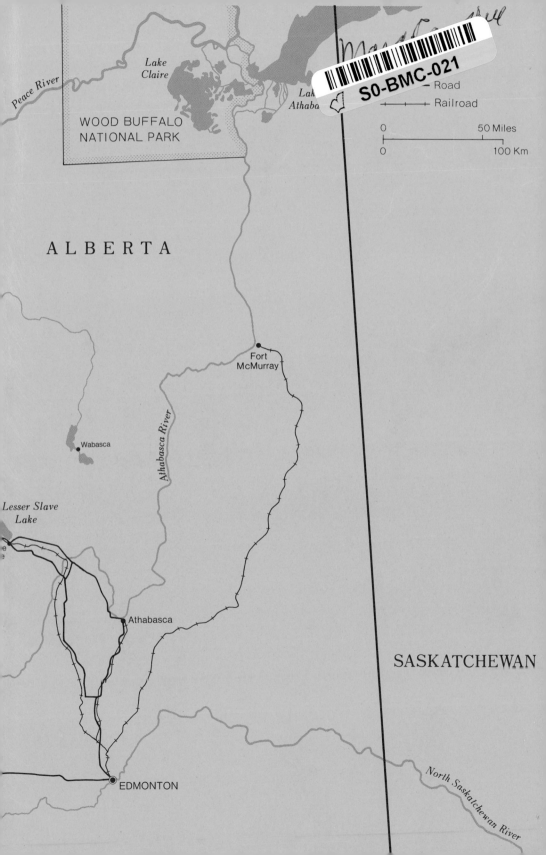

Peace River

Lake
Claire

WOOD BUFFALO
NATIONAL PARK

Lake
Athabasca

S0-BMC-021

———— Road
+—+—+— Railroad

0   50 Miles
0   100 Km

ALBERTA

Fort
McMurray

Athabasca River

Wabasca

Lesser Slave
Lake

Athabasca

SASKATCHEWAN

EDMONTON

North Saskatchewan River

Frontier Justice

The Peace River at the junction of the Peace and Smoky Rivers, near the town. (Provincial Archives of Alberta: Photograph Collection A1212.)

Frontier Justice

The Reminiscences of
Ged Baldwin

THE UNIVERSITY OF ALBERTA PRESS

First published by
The University of Alberta Press
Athabasca Hall
Edmonton, Alberta, Canada
1987

Copyright © The University of Alberta Press 1987

Canadian Cataloguing in Publication Data

Baldwin, Ged, 1907-
   Frontier justice

  ISBN 0-88864-124-9

  1. Baldwin, Ged, 1907-   2. Lawyers — Peace
River Region (B.C. and Alta.) — Biography. 3.
Trials — Peace River Region (B.C. and Alta.) —
Anecdotes, facetiae, satire, etc. 4. Peace River
Region (B.C. and Alta.) — History. 5. Peace
River Region (B.C. and Alta.) — Biography. 6.
Justice, Administration of — Peace River Region
(B.C. and Alta.) — History. I. Title.
KE416.B34A3 1987   349.7123'1'0924   C87-091448-0

All rights reserved
No part of this publication may be produced, stored in a retrieval system,
or transmitted in any form or by any means, electronic, mechanical, photocopying,
recording, or otherwise, without prior permission of the copyright owner.

Typesetting by The Typeworks, Vancouver, British Columbia, Canada

Printed by Hignell Printing Limited, Winnipeg, Manitoba, Canada

CONTENTS

Preface

THIS BOOK IS MOSTLY ABOUT THE COURTS AND THE justice they administered in northwestern Alberta during much of the first half of the twentieth century. As well, it is my attempt to tell about the land and the people of the Peace, one of the last examples in North America of a frontier area struggling to shape itself into an occupied and settled region. The Peace River area stretches all the way from the eastern slopes of the Rockies to the rising sun and to the far north. The river itself bursts through a narrow mountain passage, empties into the great central plain, then works its way north to join the Slave and Mackenzie rivers onward to the Arctic ocean. For many years the region was hardly more than a transportation corridor to the Northern Territories and the Yukon, if "corridor" can describe one or two rough land trails and summer transportation from time to time on the river.

People came through here following the overland trail to the Yukon gold rush. Some went no further; others coming back remembered the lush green country and decided to remain. The Catholic Church brought people from Quebec to settle in the Donnelly, Mclennan, Falher, and Girouxville districts. Soldiers, attracted by land grants, came after the First World War to settle in Peace River. Eager immigrants from central Europe, desperate, after years of oppression, for their own farms, their own lands, found the end of the rainbow in Peace River. Another surge of settlers came after the Second World War. Veterans with rehabilitation credits came to take up farming. Always, too, there were the restless, the solitary seekers. They came one by one, the discontented and the dispossessed with their families, driven from the last home, still willing or fool-hardy enough to keep on moving out to the very edge of human habitation. The native peoples are part of the Peace River story. They were here long before any European wandered north. Over the years, however, the Indians were pushed back, prodded,squeezed into little backwaters. They were not, I think, so much oppressed as kept out of sight—and out of mind—mislaid and forgotten.

There is a beautiful Indian legend about the Peace River and its name. Long ago two Indian tribes had been fighting against one another. Some said their battles were incited by rival trad-ing companies seeking wider fur-trading areas. In any event, tribal chiefs and their wise men decided to hold a council. They wanted the violence to stop. It was benefiting no one but the white man. The two tribes met on a plateau along the edge of the river some miles to the east of the town of Fort Vermilion. Ac-cording to the legend, the talks were successful, the chiefs smoked the peace pipe together and decided to be friends, to not war on one another "so long as the sun shall shine and the rivers flow." The spot where the meeting took place was called thereafter Peace Point. From this legend, the river has its name.

I have always thought the legend about the Peace River's name such an appropriate story for our troubled world where the wishes of ordinary people seem no longer to count. Like many who first came into the Peace River area, I thought the river was named the Peace because it moved placidly, smoothly on its appointed way. I was wrong. There was much I would learn about the river and its people as time went by.

The roads were bad, the winters long, hard, and cold; there was little cash to go around. But there were certainly com-pensations—the people and their vital spirit of friendship and pioneer co-operation. Early in my stay in the Peace, for example, I was told I need not lock my door. Trappers and homesteaders never did. It was important that a traveller lost or unable to make it home be able to get in, even if the owner were away. Twelve-foot Davis's epitaph on top of Grouard Hill overlooking the junc-tion of the Peace and Smoky rivers reflects that pioneer ethic, telling everyone who stops to read it, and many do, that Twelve-foot Davis never locked his doors against anyone.

Davis was an interesting character, originally a prospector, then a trapper and trader. He earned his name about the turn of the century, not by being twelve-feet tall or twelve-feet wide, but for having laid claim to a twelve-foot slice of land left over in a surveying dispute. Two rival companies were contesting a gold claim and Davis got the piece in the middle. His friend, Colonel James Cornwall, also known as "Peace River Jim," erected the monument to Twelve-foot Davis on top of Grouard Hill when Davis died. They had been fast friends, each promising the other that whoever died first, the other would see to his burial at that majestic lookout point over the Peace and Smoky rivers.

Sometime around 1960, I was having lunch in the sixth-floor parliamentary restaurant in the Centre Block in Ottawa, when I was called to the telephone with a message that Cyrus Eaton wanted to speak with me. Eaton was a multi-millionaire who had obtained some additional fame by opening his summer home at Pugwash, Nova Scotia, to meetings of businessmen, statesmen, and philosophers who met quite regularly to discuss important issues in science and world affairs. The place had attracted many well-known figures from all sections of the world to its meetings. I naturally wondered what this man could want of me. A brisk voice on the line connected me to Cyrus Eaton. He told me he wanted to organize an international peace centre at Peace River. It would have permanent buildings and staff to host annual meetings for people from both sides of the iron curtain. Plans were already underway for the first of these gatherings, and Eaton wanted to know if I would help. In particular, would I seek our government's co-operation for the project? Eaton added that the town's name, Peace River, had been what attracted his attention to this location for his project. I started to tell him the story of how the Peace had its name when Eaton laughed, saying, "No doubt you are right, Baldwin. I had a very complete research job done. The legend is factual." For my part, unfortunately, I was able to get little co-operation from our government for the Peace River project. In due course the scheme fell apart. But what a grand idea it would have been had it succeeded: Peace River, an international centre for peace.

As if suspended in time, the land and its people suffered less of the trauma of the world wars and the Depression. It kept intact much of the hardy good sense of the frontier.

It has been my belief for many years that a story can be told about this country and those who lived in it under the frontier's social contract of sturdy independence. This book tells part of that story. I have recounted here a number of legal trials, mostly homicide cases, with their respective backgrounds and related procedures, something of a potpourri of northern judicial proceedings as my way of telling the tale. Each trial incident stands by itself; but put together, I hope the reader will find them a fair depiction of the several generations of Northerners who ushered the Peace River area out of its pioneer days.

Acknowledgements

I WANT TO EXPRESS MY THANKS TO ALL WHO HAVE contributed to the research, writing, and editing of this book. I owe much to my wife Beulah. Beulah's research on her own Peace River pioneer heritage provoked my research for this collection of stories. Her parents came into the north country over the Athabasca trail by team and sleigh, and she is now writing that fascinating story of their epic journey to Peace River. Because many of my old files were no longer available, the officials of the attorney general's office in Edmonton and the staff of the clerk of the court in Peace River were most helpful in finding so many of the records I needed to supplement my personal recollections. The Alberta provincial archives provided additional material and photographs, as did the Alexander Mackenzie Museum at Peace River and the public relations office of the CNR. The *Peace River Record Gazette* helped me locate the stories and editorials pertaining to the Bradley murder case. I am indebted to my daughter Barbara who spent many hours advising me in the early stages of the manuscript's planning and writing, and to Maureen Korp for the final edit of the manuscript. Finally, I am most grateful for the kindness and co-operation of Norma Gutteridge and the University of Alberta Press, and my friend Professor Gerry Gall of the Law Faculty of the University of Alberta for thinking there might be some merit in these pages.

CHAPTER ONE

Frontier Justice

IT WAS THE SUMMER OF 1929 WHEN I FIRST STOPPED MY car at the top of Grouard Hill and gazed down upon the beauty of the Peace River valley. About a thousand feet below me lay the little town of Peace River on the east bank of the river. Little islands dotted the river. On the other side, a wide jack pine flat merged into the steep hills. Barely visible were the few houses comprising the community of West Peace River on the other side of the river from the town of Peace River itself. West Peace River had been a flourishing settlement once when a ferry was the only means of crossing the river, but that was before the bridge was constructed a mile downstream. The river had a wide, easy flow as it moved north beneath the sparkling, sun-filled sky. I was enchanted. This was the heart of northern Alberta's Peace River region. Although I did not know it at that moment, the rest of my life would be bound up with this beautiful land—as a lawyer, a farmer, and later as its Member of Parliament. I had come into the Peace River district only as a tourist. I was young, I was looking for adventure, and—to top everything—I was rich, at the moment.

Like so many other inhabitants of the young province of Alberta, I had not been born there. My mother had brought me from New Zealand when I was six. We were to join Dad who had come to Canada before us to establish his law practice. Initially, he opened an office in Edmonton, then in Vegreville, a town in eastern Alberta. That is where I grew up. At the age of sixteen, I entered Dad's office to read law. It seemed reasonable. I had finished school. Why not? Not long after, however, the regulations for admission to the bar in the province were changed. An applicant had now to have a university degree. In my case and for a few others still under the former practice, we were to spend five years under articles and write four examinations for which we prepared on our own. Then we could be admitted to the bar if successful in our studies.

During my first year as an articled student for my father, I was paid $15 a month. When I reported to work, he showed me five coal stoves and told me my duties included keeping them free of ashes and supplied with coal. No trace of nepotism in Dad's office for me. Eventually I progressed to more responsible duties. I was allowed to file. I distinguished myself by losing a set of valuable securities. They stayed missing in my files for ten days before I located them. I kept on, however, at my task of reading law. Dad let me sit in some trials with him, petty criminal cases and small debts. Finally, he decided I might be ready for something bigger.

He dispatched me north of Vegreville to a tiny community to appear on a preliminary inquiry for a man charged with indecent assault. I was eighteen, and I looked even younger than that. As I was about to walk into the schoolhouse, now serving as the courtroom for this inquiry, the attending policeman placed a detaining hand on my shoulder. He boomed out, "Run along, boy; children aren't allowed to go in there today." Nothing I said dissuaded him. He boomed all the more. I was forced to send for my client. *He* led me into the courtroom.

In due course, however, I passed my examinations, reached the required age of 21, and was called to the bar. I set up practice in the new town of Two Hills. There was not much money. At first, cases were few and far between. Then two years later, I was wealthy. I had gambled on wheat futures and won a paper fortune of $15,000. No one had ever told me that it was so easy to make so much money. Why work, ever? I closed up my office, bought a new car, a snappy gray roadster with blue trim and wire wheels, and I set off to see the world. My first stop would be the Peace River area of which I had read and heard so much.

I was not disappointed when I got there. Everyone I met seemed laced with a special sort of optimism. The morning after my arrival I was in the local barber shop. I could not help but express my enthusiasm for what I was seeing in the north. Someone sitting in Wyn Waldrer's chair pushed the towel aside, sat up, and said to me in a deadpan voice: "Son, you will get over that. I've been here twenty years, and in all that time, I have only known two good years—the one before I got here, and next year!" Later, we became friends. Once when I reminded him of his greeting, he grinned and said that the young need to be kept down in their proper place.

I found lodgings in the town of Peace River and for several weeks enjoyed myself as a young man of means. Then friends invited me to go off on a week-long hunting trip. When I returned, it was to paupery. The wheat market had collapsed. My net cash worth was less than $5.00. I needed a means of support, fast.

The town of Berwyn, about 25 miles from Peace River, came to my rescue. For my legal services on behalf of the town and my hockey-playing skills on behalf of the town team, they would pay me a small salary. I accepted. I opened a little law office in Berwyn. One by one other clients began to trickle in. Some even managed to pay for my services in coin of the realm. More often, my recompense was stove wood, or lumber, or crop produce, even livestock sometimes. These were, after all, the Depression years.

Several months later Charlie Roberts, a Peace River lawyer, invited me to enter his firm as a full partner. I left Berwyn. I must confess other interests were drawing me back to Peace River. I had become engaged to Beulah Freeland. She was the daughter of Peace River homesteaders, who had come north over the Athabasca trail by horse-drawn sleigh in the winter of 1913. She was the best-looking girl in the district, and was also the hockey fan who had yelled the loudest for my blood when Peace River played the Berwyn hockey team.

I stayed in the north. It was a place to call home. Peace River is a unique, distinct land—economically, socially, geographically. In 1930 the town of Peace River was probably about 700 strong. Because the ferry service over the river was there, the town itself had been called Peace River Crossing, or simply the "Crossing." The ferry service made it at once the distribution, administrative, and municipal centre for a vast inland area of bush, prairie, lake, and river that stretched west to the border of British Columbia and north to the Northwest Territories. Alexander Mackenzie had wintered just ten miles upriver at Fort Fork 140 years earlier. Only now, however, was Peace River beginning to develop into a frontier agricultural community. It was in many ways a very young town. The railroad from the south had been pushing ahead by fits and starts for years as part of the planned overland transportation route to the Yukon and the Northwest Territories. By 1915, steel rail had reached Mclennan where it divided. One branch went west to the Smoky River; another, the northerly line, went to Reno about 20 miles southeast of the town of Peace River. As the rail line progressed, small settlements, villages, towns appeared along the way. These little settlements, along with the outpouring of dollars for the construction of the rail line, drew more settlers, business people, and professionals. This was one of the last frontier areas anywhere. There were, too, plenty of colorful, raffish types, the old-timers. It was my privilege to know many of these characters. I heard exciting, far-fetched, splendid yarns from them about the beginning of the town, the settlements, the conflicts and the neighborliness, the common culture of finding, exploring, and settling a new land.

There was a Peace River judicial district, located in the town of Peace River. We had a small courthouse with a courtroom of minute proportions. Court offices, the clerk, and the sheriff were all located here. A small block of cells over at the RCMP barracks served as the district jail. Under provincial law, sentences not exceeding two months could be served in the district. More than that, and the culprit must be sent off to the provincial jail at Fort Saskatchewan, not far from Edmonton. One of the district jail cells was also used as an interview room. I first met and interviewed many of the men and women who were to go on trial for their lives in that airless little basement cell.

The police authority was headquartered in Peace River also. Their offices, barracks, and commanding officer's residence were located beside the river at the town's southern limits. The Royal Northwest Mounted Police, or RNWMP, was the original force. For a few years, they were replaced by the Alberta Provincial Police. Then the federal force resumed control with a new name, the Royal Canadian Mounted Police, our familiar RCMP today. One of the first commissioners of Alberta's provincial force was Major A.E.C. Macdonnell. He had been once the superintendent of the "N" division of the RNWMP. Upon his retirement from that force, he joined the provincial, and when he retired from the provincial, he became the police magistrate at Peace River. I tried many cases before the Major, as he was always called. I did not win many. He was a kindly and courteous gentleman, and seemingly well-disposed toward me; but like many policemen who become magistrates, the Major believed in the infallibility of the police. When the criminal code and the laws of evidence did not square precisely with the case for the Crown, the Major had no difficulty gently pushing the law to one side.

I remember one occasion when I conducted what I thought to be a reasonably successful cross-examination of a constable. Macdonnell turned to me and said, "Mr. Baldwin, this will not really do your client any good. I know the RCMP and its officers. They never pick on an innocent man. If your client was not guilty, he would not be in the prisoner's dock today." Well, of course, this set me back. But there was no use kicking up a fuss. His worship quite honestly believed this. My client was convicted and fined. The fine was heavy enough, however, to warrant an appeal I was able to win in a higher court. I often won the appeals I took from Macdonnell's court.

Now I quite recognize the imperfections of the law, but the principle set out by the Major in his remarks is not a safe guide upon which to rest decisions of innocence or guilt.

In the early days, even up to the time of my arrival in Peace River, the police subdivision had less than 40 officers, NCOs, and constables to police an area comprising the entire northwest quarter of the province. Communication was limited, roads even worse. With few exceptions, the police were good policemen. They were seldom abrasive and had the support of the local communities. In magistrate's court, I invariably acted for the defence, while RCMP officers, particularly detachment NCOs, usually conducted the prosecution. Despite our many battles over the years, I remained on friendly terms with most of these men. This is a far cry from today. The irregular, and at times illegal, tactics of the "James Bond" sorts in security have truly marred the record of the RCMP.

When there were trials with wide public interest, such as murder cases, we could not use our little courtroom because it was never large enough to accommodate all the spectators.

Church halls were sometimes big enough. The United Church was once used with the pulpit serving as a witness box, although that did not deter the usual amount of perjury one whit. The local movie theatre was another substitute courtroom at times. I recall one very emotional scene when the jury brought in a verdict of guilty. The accused, a lad of nineteen, was told to stand to receive sentence. As he rose to his feet, he collapsed. Two constables were needed to support him. His sobs rang out in the crowded and deathly still theatre. The judge pronounced the grim words of the sentence, " . . . to be hanged by the neck until you are dead." As I stood beside that boy, I could see the commercial signs of local merchants painted on the theatre curtain. It was so incongruous as to be indecent.

A few years later I was counsel for a storekeeper from a small community on Slave Lake. As we entered the church engaged for the day's proceedings, my client, the plaintiff in a divorce case, whispered to me, "Mr. Baldwin, isn't this the old United Church?" I told him it was and he shook his head. "I guess not many people can say they were divorced in the same church where they were married. My wife and I stood up in this very church twenty years ago to be married."

The trial division of the supreme court, which had unlimited jurisdiction in both civil and criminal matters, usually held two sittings a year in Peace River, so all important cases had to be delayed until a judge of the high court could come north. This sometimes meant discriminatory treatment for people committed for criminal trial if their circumstances did not permit them to make bail. They simply stayed in jail until a judge came to try the case. Often the accused spent several months in custody. If ultimately found innocent, it was just too bad.

When the docket had criminal trials listed, a number of potential jurors would be summoned. Usually court authorities attempted to limit the jury panel to men living in and around the town in order to avoid problems of extra expense and the nuisance of hotel accommodations. Thus, over the years, a town man might serve on several juries. This was a matter of importance to counsel. We would spend hours poring over the list, attempting to secure background information on potential jurymen—their habits, histories, domestic backgrounds, their approaches to social issues. Living in the town itself and know-

ing most of the people was a big plus for an
Sometimes we would hear tidbits about view
and-so concerning an upcoming case. That cc
useful to us. It gave the counsel a solid base fc
man whose name was drawn. The lawyers w
River had a distinct, and I think a proper, ad
Crown in this regard. The Crown could appr
ample funds, could bring witnesses in from a
world, could have the police fetch and carry and
investigations on its behalf, but we knew the tov
be called to jury duty.

So far as the defence was concerned, I have to s
general was usually miserly. I conducted a great r
tal cases both as Crown-appointed and paid co
paid by the attorney general for my services wa
than $150. This had to cover the inquest, prelim
and the trial, not to mention days travelling a distr
ing witnesses, and painstakingly attempting to ob
local feelings. In many instances I fought losing b
suade the Crown to pay witness expenses for an
did not have a nickle to his name and had been in
time awaiting trial.

Once a man had actually been sworn on a jury,
proper and illegal for him to discuss the case even
over, but in small communities people are always m
talking. Those who had done jury duty would som
me, years later, of the basis for a jury's decision. I was
prised at the seemingly insignificant details which
"six good men and true" to find the verdict they did, a
was also often heartened by the basic and fundamental
sense which went into the result. I remember, howe
glaring exception.

I was awaiting my turn to try a case in a small northei
The case preceding mine was a murder trial. Although I
involved, I sat in the courtroom anyway to listen. In my
the facts did not justify a conviction for murder. Neverth
had been a particularly brutal drunken brawl brought to a
conclusion when several rowdies threw their victim
ground and kicked him in the head, causing concussion
death. The trial judge wanted a murder conviction. The (

cutor, who might well have worked out a guilty plea for
laughter, refused to reduce the charge. The trial was thus
ed several days and the annoyed jurymen kept in atten-
e. After the evidence was in and counsel made their respec-
addresses, the judge, having worked himself into quite a
gave his directions, virtually ordering the jury to convict.
ainly everyone expected the verdict, at the very minimum,
ld be manslaughter. The jury was out briefly. When they re-
ed the foreman stood up, looked the judge defiantly in the
and to the amazement of all said, "Not guilty." The judge,
riated, dismissed the jury, but not without a tongue lash-

efore returning to Peace River, I found out what had hap-
ed. Most of the jury were farmers, and this was harvest time.
en they discovered a manslaughter plea would have ended
whole matter several days earlier, they took out their anger
inst "those SOBs from outside" by letting the accused off.
Unlike supreme court justices, judges of the district court
ne into our district quite frequently and sat in centres other
an the two main towns of Peace River and Grande Prairie. We
ere always improvising suitable accommodations for the dig-
ty of the learned judges and the solemnity of the judicial pro-
edings. It is not easy to reflect the awful majesty of the law in a
y-infested, dusty dance hall still decorated for the party the
ight before. Once we held court in a Legion hall. We used the
yer, not visible from the judge's bench, as a lawyer's robing
oom. In attendance that day was an older member of the bar.
His fondness for the bottle had earned him a fiery red nose and
he nickname "Rudolph." Rudolph was suffering the ill effects
of a bad night. He was making heavy weather of the case, often
osing the thread of the argument and confusing the witness.
Finally he said he was feeling most unwell and requested a brief
adjournment. Rudolph went off to the robing room. From where
we sat at the counsel table, we were able to watch our learned
friend, in full view of the public, pull a bottle of rye from his old-
fashioned bag, and take several slugs. He then put the bottle
back in the bag, adjusted his gown, and returned to carry on the
battle with a beatific smile and enough energy to finish the case.

I always thought the arbitrary division between district and
supreme courts stupid and invidious. As a bencher of the law

society and later as a Member of Parliament, I made several propositions to bring it to an end. It is an idiotic theory that because a supreme court judge is paid a higher salary and was then called "My Lord" instead of "Your Honor," his judgment is worth more. I do not believe the district court made any more errors in its findings than the supreme court.

In the north where transportation was such a vital link with the rest of the world, it was always something of an event to watch the weekly train pull in from the south. But even more interesting was to be at the Hudson's Bay landing when the *D.A. Thomas* arrived and discharged her passengers. They were always a mixed and interesting group—fur buyers, trappers, Bay people, priests and nuns, an occasional homesteader, possibly a Mountie escorting a prisoner to jail, and now and then, a government official from Edmonton or Ottawa, who always occupied the most expensive and comfortable accommodations, at government expense, of course. The *D.A. Thomas* was the main vessel in the Bay fleet until 1930. She was a large, wood-burning, paddle wheeler. The boat could accommodate many passengers, had a commodious dining room, and comfortable staterooms. Passengers who did not have the price of a bed could spread their bedrolls and sleep on deck. Freight was mostly carried in scows pushed in tandem by the boat. Her fuel consumption was fairly hefty, especially when the river was high. At various places along the river, wood was cut and piled for her use. The pilot would simply nose the boat to shore and pick up fuel when it was needed.

From spring thaw to freeze-up, virtually all transport for passengers and freight travelled by water via Peace River Crossing. Peace River was the chief river port in the area for all commercial craft, not just the Hudson's Bay Company boats, bringing supplies in to the outlying areas and taking furs, grain, and livestock back out. In winter a few trails led between Peace River and Fort Vermilion some 200 miles north. Between Peace River Crossing and Fort Vermilion, the only other settlement was one trading post—Carcajou—and a few scattered trappers' cabins.

Once in a while, there would be several trials involving people in and around Fort Vermilion. If they were important enough and if it were the summer season, a judicial party might be assembled—judge, lawyers, court officials, police, expert witnesses—all would gather to carry the justice of the "Great White Father" to the inhabitants of the north. The rationale behind these judicial junkets was twofold: One, to expose the people of Fort Vermilion to the law and let them watch its pageantry unfold—the judge seated high on the dais, the coat of arms, the officials in their gowns, the Mounties in their red tunics. Secondly, it saved the expense of bringing witnesses, litigants, and the accused to Peace River. If judges and officials wanted to enjoy a break in the droning monotony of a more civilized court routine further south, this was a bonus.

A trial was once held in the *D.A. Thomas*'s dining salon during a two-day journey to Fort Vermilion. Charlie Roberts, my Peace River law partner for so many years, was counsel for the plaintiff. Most of his witnesses were at Fort Vermilion. The defence counsel had most of his people on board the *D.A. Thomas* with him. Anxious to impress the other passengers, the defence counsel offered to put in his defence before the plaintiff made his case. One after the other, he put his witnesses on the stand, then submitted them for cross-examination. He made such a botch of the case, and Roberts conducted such a skilful cross-examination, that before the boat docked in Fort Vermilion, the judge announced the defence had established the case for the plaintiff and gave judgment to the plaintiff for the full amount claimed, plus costs. When Roberts' client came down to the boat to meet his lawyer, he learned he had won the case already!

Mr. Justice Walsh, a great gentleman and fine lawyer, who was later to become lieutenant governor of Alberta, began his career in the Yukon. He enjoyed taking the Peace River circuit because several of his old Yukon cronies now lived in Peace River. In 1930 he appointed me defence counsel for a hearing in Fort Vermilion. The list had two criminal actions and a civil trial for which no defence counsel were named. In his judgment, the cases were of sufficient importance to warrant his asking me to take on the job. Judge Walsh added, with a twinkle in his eye, "I am afraid it won't be very financially rewarding, Baldwin. The attorney general had indicated he will pay your expenses and a grant fee of $25."

It certainly was not a lot of money. The whole trip would take at least a week. But this was 1930. I was young, and the adventure of a boat trip to colorful Fort Vermilion appealed to me. I gladly accepted. The next Sunday, I embarked on the *M.V. Buffalo Lakes,* a smaller vessel which had replaced the *D.A. Thomas* the previous summer.

It was a delightful trip. Judge Walsh presided with humor and dignity at the dining table. His favorite court reporter, Mr. Barnett, was also aboard. Mr. Barnett was the father of Tim Barnett, who would follow his father's lead to become Alberta's chief court reporter. Mr. Barnett was an entertaining chap with numerous stories of his court experiences. The time travelling went all too quickly.

We made our way north without running aground and, arriving in Fort Vermilion, tied up at the Hudson's Bay landing. The boat would be our home during our stay. The river is fairly wide at this point. Across the river, on the north banks, lay North Vermilion, site of the Bay's corporate rival, the Revillon Frères trading post. Fort Vermilion was strung out along the southern bank. Within this thin band were trappers' cabins and other houses interspersed with the Roman Catholic church, convent, and dormitories, the Anglican church, the Hudson's Bay post, the RCMP station, schools, and several other places of business.

There was quite a lot of small boat activity. The trapping season had just finished, and crowds of natives were bringing their furs to sell. Some had brought in their dog teams, leaving them staked along the banks where small dog houses had been built. The native trappers were quiet, soft-spoken men, who carried themselves with dignity. I saw no traces of drinking or fighting. Having disposed of their furs, most would pay out their grub-stakes, buy new supplies, and return to their cabins by boat or trail. I do not mean to suggest all was well with these people; there was sickness and hardship, particularly in a bad season. Yet, in my opinion, their life had to be far better than the lives of those sequestered in the bush slums that were the result of the ill-starred school experiments generated by the federal Department of Indian and Northern Affairs. Progress had to come to the north, yes; nevertheless, the federal bureaucracy has a lot to answer for in the shoddy meddling they exercised there.

Court was held in the old Diamond P store and post, one of the few buildings big enough to hold the courtroom fixtures and a large number of residents. Several hundred locals usually came to watch and listen. There was absolutely no other form of entertainment in the settlement in those days to compete with a live trial. People unable to jam into the building itself would gather at the doorway.

We decided the criminal cases did not warrant a jury. This simplified and speeded our proceedings. The afternoon following our arrival, Mrs. Carlisle, the clerk of the court, stood before the judge's bench in her black gown and called out, "Oyez. Oyez. All who have business before the King's supreme court, gather near and be heard." The wheels of justice began to turn.

The most unusual case involved a charge of aggravated assault against a clergyman, who was also a farmer, for beating a young servant boy severely. Inquiries made locally confirmed the opinion I had gained earlier from reading the preliminary inquiry depositions—namely, the man had a vile temper. He had assaulted the lad with a stick and injured him severely enough to put the lad in the hospital. There was no defence possible. I advised the man to plead guilty so that more sordid facts would not have to be aired. My advice was summarily rejected. The accused seemed to feel he did not need a lawyer, certainly not some jumped-up young squirt from Peace River. He informed me with an air of arrogant indifference he must plead "not guilty." He wanted all the facts brought out. He hinted he had really been engaged in God's work. Under different circumstances, I would have given up my brief. However, I kept my temper and did the best I could for my client. He insisted upon giving evidence. In his defence, the clergyman quoted his version of scripture as to the right of a master to discipline his servant. Only the Lord could punish him.

Mr. Justice Walsh resisted the temptation to interrupt and waited until the accused was finished. He informed him then that here, on earth, in Canada, in matters covered by the criminal code, he was, by law, the judge. Then, citing scripture as well as the criminal code, Judge Walsh found the accused guilty. Because the clergyman had a family, he was not sent to jail, but was fined, put on probation, and ordered to pay damages, including the lad's hospital costs.

Since that first trip I travelled often to the Fort. Business and politics, including the campaign in connection with the building of the Peace River-to-Pine Point railway, made me a frequent visitor; however, that first trip stands out in my mind as no other. Many years later I was reminded of the clergyman's case when I read of another trial: The accused wound up a lengthy and flamboyant defence statement in court by thundering, "As God is my judge, I am not guilty." The judge's concise retort was, "*He* is not, *I* am, *you* are."

Another judge who enjoyed taking the northern circuit was Mr. Justice Tweedie. Judge Tweedie was a member of a prominent New Brunswick family. He was a big, burly, sentimental man, who had difficulty keeping his sentimental side under control when forced to pronounce a death sentence. One week he tried three murder cases in town. All were difficult and we were glad when it was over. Tweedie signalled the end of court by throwing a party in his hotel. Almost everyone who had participated in the trials came—the lawyers, police, court officials, the witnesses, both defence and Crown. I believe even a few jurors came by.

Judges like Walsh and Tweedie, I believe, were men with an understanding of the people they dealt with. They usually managed to mix justice with sympathy and equity. No one was a match in that regard, however, to Judge Noel. Judge Noel was one of the first French-Canadian judges to take the northern circuit. He once acquitted a homesteader who had been accused of stealing a pig. The facts in evidence made it absolutely plain the offence had been proven. The man had stolen the pig to feed his family. When the Crown prosecutor took exception to the acquittal, Noel replied, "But it was such a little pig." This was the same judge who, when told a certain judgment he was about to make was contrary to the law, said lightly, "Then I jump over the law."

On the other hand it was a fact of life that some jurists did not take kindly to being sent north. They were often impatient to rush through the docket and get back to Edmonton or Calgary. To accomplish this, they would push and manipulate lawyers to hurry cases. Sometimes they would suggest that settlements be made out of court. A favorite gambit in civil actions was to hint that if there were not a settlement and the case were tried to the bitter end, costs might be limited or not awarded at all.

One night as I sat in my office trying to prepare a rough and sticky murder case and wishing I had more time in which to do it, there was a rap on my door. In walked the court reporter, clearly at that hour of the night an emissary from the judge. The court reporter mentioned that my case was likely to take a week. He also noted another case, considered several weeks earlier, seemed similar. The accused, whose mental condition was in doubt, was not compelled to proceed with his trial until a psychiatric survey of his ability to plead had been held. The court reporter mentioned further that he thought it was pretty obvious to everyone, including the judge, that my client was a doubtful mental case. A wink being as good as a nod, I raised the subject of my client's mental condition in court the next morning. The judge briskly agreed a psychiatric assessment was in order, overruled the prosecutor's angry objections, and rushed to catch the train. His bags were already packed and waiting. I now had much-needed time to prepare a proper defence.

The foot soldiers of Alberta's judicial system, particularly in the north, were the police magistrates and justices of the peace. They issued summons and warrants, heard preliminary inquiries, and summary criminal proceedings. It was in the magistrate's courts that the vast majority of people came up against the system of criminal justice for matters such as liquor law violations; offences against game and fishing regulations, and vehicle and traffic laws; prostitution; vagrancy; common assault, and petty theft. In the beginning magistrates and justices of the peace were appointed from the ranks of retired police officers, businessmen, and farmers of standing in the community. There were no salaries. Those men presiding were compensated on a fee basis for each case. In some instances, payment was available only from costs collected from the people found guilty and fined. Thus there was considerable pressure on the bench to presume the accused guilty, not innocent until proven guilty beyond a reasonable doubt, because of the profit motive.

I once defended a man found guilty of making moonshine. The local justice, a small shopkeeper and farmer, lived in a community not far from Peace River. There was absolutely no evidence to support the finding. Even the constable looked a little thunderstruck at the verdict. I jumped up angrily to denounce the judgment, saying, "I will not stand for this! I will appeal it!"

His worship gave me a hard look, took his seat again, then said, "All right, Mr. Baldwin. I will hear your appeal now."

Magistrate's court was held in all sorts of improbable places—a homesteader's shack, the trading post, or community building, a one-room schoolhouse. I once attended a hearing on the roadway by the side of a car. Frequently the accused was not represented by counsel. He simply told his story and trusted to luck. Magistrates also heard preliminary inquiries into more serious criminal matters. However, in those situations, the accused could exercise their right for trial by a higher court, including a jury trial. In the main, I believe the early magistrates and justices did a pretty good job despite their lack of formal legal training. Their knowledge of local conditions and of the people, plus a good measure of pioneer common sense, made them an invaluable element of the justice of the north. The system did work. Charlie Roberts passed on a story to me years ago that well illustrates this point.

It involved a Fort Vermilion trapper. He had taken a boat to cross the river and failed to return it to its owner. The justice who tried the case had access only to an ancient English law book belonging to the Bay manager. Anxious to adhere to the tradition of good British common law, the justice went through the book carefully. He decided the charge best fitting the crime was "piracy on the high seas." The culprit was duly charged and found guilty. Reading further in the law book to find out what the sentence should be, both the justice and the constable were horrified to learn the mandatory punishment for piracy was execution by hanging. With typical pioneer ingenuity, however, they found a solution to do Solomon proud. The justice imposed sentence—death by hanging—then suspended it.

The few of us at the bar in those days did the major share of criminal defence. We were constantly in magistrate's court. Even when we had the option of electing for trial by a higher court, we usually settled for the magistrate's court. There were good reasons for that. We had the benefit of local knowledge in the magistrate; we were pretty certain a conviction would bring a lower penalty or a fine with time to pay it off; and we knew we could always appeal the decision if our strategy failed. Compared to all of that was the danger of the higher court's judicial lottery. If we asked for a trial by judge, just who would be sent up from Edmonton or Calgary?

Like many of the professional people who came north, the early lawyers were a mixed bag. Some were men of impeccable academic qualifications, who had come to grief early in their careers—mostly because of drink. There were also those who were somewhat iconoclastic, they just felt more comfortable on the edge of settlement. And there was the very rare type, my partner, Charlie Roberts. Charlie fell between both stools.

C.J. Roberts was an Irishman, a solicitor from Belfast. His laconic account of how he happened to come to North America is well worth repeating here. Charlie and some boon companions had gone to the pier in Belfast to bid farewell to a friend sailing for New York. The wine and the whiskey flowed freely. Charlie had just "one more drink" after the "all ashore" had been sounded. When he awakened the next morning, he was nursing a gorgeous hangover and was 200 miles or so on his way to New York City. There was nothing else to do but continue onward. His friend went good for his passage; and Charlie, upon arrival in the New World, liked what he saw. He cabled home for more money and decided to stay on a bit. He worked as a law clerk for a while in New York, then moved on to Winnipeg. Eventually, Charlie drifted west to the new town of Edson, Alberta. By then Charlie's drinking problem was serious. When the construction boom played out, Charlie went north to Peace River. Here he stayed until he died. He had stopped drinking some years before I met him, but the damage had been done to his system. He never really recovered from the effects of his earlier alcoholism.

Charlie Roberts had the wit of the Irish. He had a fine sense of humor, was a voracious reader, and a great student of the law and of humanity. Above all, he had an inimitable capability for judging human nature. This gift made him one of the best and most nimble practitioners of the fine art of cross-examination. Although the leading barrister in the north, he had no patience with pretension. He preferred the rough and plain talk of a trapper to that of any visiting élite.

The years I spent working with Charlie as a partner were valuable ones. Charlie always knew exactly when to stop questioning the witness, thus avoiding the fatal error common to so many counsel—asking one more question and by it putting your client's head in the noose. I learned much from him.

Charlie Roberts could have been the leader at the bar wherever he lighted. He lived and died in the north, in the land he loved, among the people he knew best, the people who placed their trust so often in the skill and honesty of one who was their friend as well as their lawyer.

CHAPTER TWO

Shooting in the Jack Pines

THIS STORY HAS ITS BEGINNING IN A TOWN NEAR Denver, Colorado, in July 1914, a few weeks before the beginning of the First World War. A lively and good-looking young girl, 16 years old, lived there with her mother, stepfather, and stepsister. The girl was to inherit a good sum of money when she was 18. She was stubborn and wayward, eager to enter the world outside her small community and newly engaged to a young man in the district when Ralph Bradley appeared on the scene and began to court her.

Bradley was in his late 20s or early 30s. Edith's parents did not approve of the relationship. At first their only means of communication was through a discreet exchange of notes and surreptitious telephone calls. The emotions and feelings which developed between them were patently of a different sort for each. Bradley felt a strong affection for the young, pretty, high-spirited girl; however, she was probably more attracted to the idea of being set free from a narrow family circle than to him.

Within a few weeks of their meeting, they eloped to Wyoming where they were married. From Wyoming they travelled north to Montana to the home of Bradley's family near Butte. But their honeymoon was a short one. The law caught up with the pair and Bradley was arrested on a kidnapping charge by reason of the girl's age. Edith was returned to her home, and proceedings were undertaken to have the marriage annulled, which was to have some result later. About four weeks later Bradley, who had escaped from custody or somehow been freed from the kidnapping charges, reappeared in Colorado and the two slipped away once more, returning to his home in Montana. Edith's parents must have decided to accept the relationship because no further attempt was made to separate them.

That winter, in January 1915, we find the Bradleys on the move again, this time north across the border into Canada and then to the Peace River country. We do not know why they moved. Certainly it was not to better themselves financially. The young woman either had money of her own or an allowance from her mother. My speculation is that there were hidden chapters in Bradley's earlier life which persuaded him to quit his native land and head for the frontier.

The railroad had not yet reached the town of Peace River. The most northern end of steel was some fifteen miles east of Judah on the eastern side of the valley. The Peace River railway bridge had not been constructed, and the only means of crossing the river was by ferry in the summer and ice road during the winter. Although the main section of the town was on the east bank of the river, West Peace River was a sizable community with several places of business. Located near the ferry's western terminus was a general store operated and owned by J.D. Levesque.

Shortly after arriving in Peace River, Ralph Bradley obtained a position clerking at the Levesque store and he and his wife found rooms in a house nearby, close to the ferry landing. A man called Fred Blair had a barber shop in the same building. Uphill, several miles northwest of the community, was a sawmill operated by an old-timer, W.E. Smith, his wife, and their son, Harold. Like his father, Harold was tall, strongly built, and handsome. Years later I did some legal work for W.E. Smith and got to know him quite well. By that time he was the owner of a sash and door factory and a retail lumber outlet. He was a quiet man and not disposed to idle talk. Even in his mid-seventies, he was an imposing and powerfully built figure.

In 1915 the country was still policed by the Royal Northwest Mounted Police, the RNWMP. The force's subdivisional headquarters were located on the east side of the river. The commanding officer was the legendary Inspector "Andy" Anderson, one of the great characters of the north. Andy spent most of his service in the north, and even named his daughter "Peace" Anderson after the river. When his retirement came due, he stayed on and was a familiar figure around town, particularly in the Legion.

Anderson loved to play both bridge and chess, as did I. We enjoyed many games at the CNR colonization office, located next to my office in the centre of town.

My offices consisted of three long, narrow rooms set in tandem, each heated by an old-fashioned, air-tight stove, a type in wide usage in the north at that time. The stoves were easy to start, used firewood of which we had an ample supply, and could build a pretty good heat, but, as old-timers will recall, they did not provide good circulation. It could take several hours to bring warmth to the extent of a building such as mine. Consequently, on cold winter mornings I would arrive at the office around 9:00 or 10:00 a.m., start the three fires, then scuttle next door to the CNR colonization office. Our group would gather for bridge or chess and stick to it all morning. Very rarely would I get a client in the morning unless someone was in the police cell. In that case, there would be a telephone call, and I could hear the ringing even next door. By noon, my place would be cozy and the ink in the inkwell thawed. All in all it was a pleasant way to practice law as I look back on those days more than 50 years ago.

Those cold winter mornings provided good reason to spend time in the company of Andy. He was a veritable motherlode of information about the pioneer days of the north, the early courts, and criminal law. The inspector's mustache would bristle with outrage as he recalled his long duel with the notorious Baldy Red, the will-of-the-wisp bootlegger who always managed to keep just one step ahead of the law. Andy would grin, however, when he told about the time Baldy was able to sneak a big load of whiskey into the country by hiding it among the effects of two nuns. They were new to the area and did not know the facts of life about the kind man who had been so helpful during their long trip north by wagon. Then there was the grisly anecdote Andy told when he was required to bring proof of the existence of a corpse to police headquarters down south. With no way to transport the body in winter, Andy strode into the office of his superior with the head wrapped in a container.

There were other yarns about his trips by dogteam into the bush to investigate or arrest, or his expeditions by boat to the north as far as Fort Vermilion and the many trials with which he had been involved one way or another. His favorite story, which he would tell and retell with vivid and explicit description, was of the bootlegging trial at which his old friend and my law partner, Charlie Roberts, was defence counsel. At the time commissioned police officers were often gazetted as justices of the peace, and Anderson was sitting as a justice to try this case.

In this early period, it was not necessary to prove the alcoholic content of a liquor by chemical analysis. It was sufficient merely to use the senses—smell, taste, effect and so on.

The bottle with the liquid was clearly established to have been found in the possession of the accused. The only issue was the nature, quality, and effect of the exhibit. The prosecutor insisted the liquid was intoxicating. Roberts stoutly asserted it was not. The way Charlie Roberts told the story Anderson suggested Roberts, recognized as an accomplished drinker, take a snort and give his expert opinion. Charlie was happy to comply. One drink later, he still denied the liquid was an intoxicant. He suggested Anderson have a sample to confirm his opinion. This kept on until the bottle was empty and, there being no evidence, the somewhat befuddled parties agreed the charge must be dismissed. Now Anderson's version of the story had Charlie consulting with his client after the first drink to induce him to change his plea to guilty. In the meantime, the court continued on with another case. When Charlie's case was called, the court found Charlie and his client had polished off the exhibit. However, Charlie, all Irish charm, said he had talked the matter over with his client and, as both agreed the liquid was sufficiently intoxicating to qualify, the client would change his plea to guilty!

The point of these stories is that as the police inspector, as well as being a well-liked resident of the community, Anderson kept his finger on the pulse of local activities, and he played an important role in the Bradley murder investigation and trial.

Ralph Bradley and his wife spent the winter of 1915 well enough. They met people, made new friends, were invited to parties, dances, and other social activities. Their popularity was probably due more to Edith than to her husband. She was vivacious, pretty, friendly. He was described as having a "very watchful and wary approach."

When spring comes after a hard, long northern winter the snow piles dwindle, then run off, the wide river comes free from its girdle of rough ice, the first crocuses bloom, spirits lift, hearts lighten. Trappers straggle in from their lines. Farmers and homesteaders come to town for spring planting supplies. Friendships are revived. Sometimes love appears.

In April 1915 the Bradleys met the Smith family. They were spending the weekend in town. Before too long Edith Bradley and Harold Smith were fascinated with one another.

There was one particular weekend when the two families were together at various houses for parties on Friday, Saturday, and Sunday. It was then that Harold began paying a great deal of attention to Mrs. Bradley and very clearly she did not discourage him. That Sunday Mrs. Smith, obviously at Harold's instigation, invited the girl to visit the mill the following Tuesday.

Until that point there is nothing to indicate there had been bad feeling or quarrels between the Bradleys. Most definitely there was no sign of physical abuse. Yet the facts indicate Bradley's feelings for his wife were growing stronger while any affection on her part was dwindling. She had used him to escape from the narrow confinement of her home to the outside world and any emotions she had for him were loose and shallow. I doubt if she was ever in love with him, even at the start of the relationship. Probably without being aware of it, she had wanted out of the marriage and Smith's obvious admiration and interest now awakened her to it. Bradley must have been aware of the mutual attraction between his wife and Harold Smith because his jealousy provoked a bitter quarrel just prior to her visit to the mill. First Bradley told her he did not want her to go. Edith said she would. He then ordered her to be home before nightfall. Edith replied, "I'm going out to the Smith's place and I'll stay overnight if I feel like it."

Here I have quoted the words exactly as they were taken by officials who reported the inquest and the preliminary hearing, and from the police statements which were taken down in narrative form. This type of reporting rarely does justice to the actual comments of a person questioned, but the emotional quality and human impact of the Bradley story has by no means been entirely lost in the antiseptic thin, dry language of the court and official documents. It appears from the records that the exchange between husband and wife was hot and intense and surely laid the foundation for the subsequent tragedy.

In April 1915 Edith Bradley was barely seventeen, full of life and seeking fun and excitement. She had been living with Bradley for about ten months. He was morose, moody, secretive and possessive, small in size, not particularly attractive, and much older. By contrast Harold Smith was just three or four years older than the girl, tall, handsome, and socially very congenial. They had been at parties together, had danced, played cards and felt a mutual attraction.

At the time, however, especially in the north, the sanctity of marriage was highly regarded, at least on the surface. Wife stealing was frowned upon, and divorce not readily accepted. Were the Bradleys married or not? The marriage had been annulled the previous year. Was the annulment recognized in Canada? Had there been another marriage?

Throughout the proceedings of Ralph Bradley's trial reference is made to "Mrs. Bradley." The same reference appears in various legal and official documents and in police records. On the other hand, Edith was called as a witness by the Crown to give evidence against Ralph Bradley during his trial for the murder of Harold Smith. In Canada the general rule is that neither husband nor wife can be a witness against a spouse in a criminal matter. As far as the community was concerned, the two were a properly married couple, but the girl must have had some reason for believing she was not legally tied to Bradley, and this would certainly have influenced her judgment and actions. Thus, it is easy to believe that when the girl made her defiant statement—"I'm going out to the Smith's place and I'll stay overnight if I feel like it"—she meant to give a declaration of independence; further, Bradley knew it.

Edith left home that Tuesday for the Smith mill and did not return until well into the afternoon of the next day. Because there was some anxiety about Bradley's reaction, Mrs. Smith made a point of accompanying her to town. In fact, a furious Bradley was waiting for his wife at home, demanding an explanation of why she had spent the night at the Smiths'. She responded with spirit: "I just felt like staying. And then, Mrs. Smith asked me."

Bradley, although deeply resentful, kept his temper and said little more. The girl however had the bit between her teeth. She went on to say she was going to visit her cousin, a Mr. Findley who lived in the Round Lake region. It was obvious, however, she did not intend to go to Findley's. She was returning to

Harold Smith's home at the mill. Bradley, suspecting this, said, "If you go to Findley's, I'm going too." She replied, "What about your job? How can you go? Anyway if you do, you'll have to pay your own way. I'm sick and tired of having to pay out money for your expenses."

Later that day she went to the Levesque store where her husband was working and found him writing a letter about her to Findley. He asked, "What shall I put in this letter?" She responded, "I don't care what you put in it or what you tell Findley. I'm going anyway." He questioned, "Do you love me?" Her reply was, "No! And if I want to go to Round Lake I will, and I will only come back if *I* wish."

Bradley then told her she must make her final decision then and there and that if she left it would be for good. Flinging at him that she had already made up her mind and was getting out of town that day, she left the store.

That evening, without seeing Ralph again, Edith packed her things. When she left her home and husband and headed for the mill she did not go alone. She went with Harold Smith. He had also come into town that afternoon. Earlier he went to the Levesque store and asked to speak to Ralph. The two men talked privately for a short time. Then Smith left, went to the Bradley house, picked up Edith, and drove her to his place. Harold, with the brashness of the young, must have told Bradley he was taking the girl with him, and just as certainly, Bradley must have warned Smith to leave her alone—advice the young man would have done well to have heeded. But young and impetuous, he could not have taken the older man seriously. His superiority in strength and size made him supremely confident; he had nothing to fear from Bradley! He forgot, as have so many others, that a gun in the hands of a man who knows how to use it, is willing to do so, and capable of finding the opportunity, is a great equalizer.

During the rest of the spring and into the summer, the Bradleys remained apart—he living in town and still working at the store, she staying at the mill with the Smiths. In a small isolated community like Peace River it was only natural that the Smith-Bradley triangle was often commented on and, as will appear, Bradley's activity helped to promote this interest. In the main, public sympathy was with Bradley because he was the injured husband. There was also an undercurrent of feeling against the Smith family in the town. Bradley brooded over his wrongs, his rage growing as his attempts to persuade his wife to return home were continually frustrated. On several occasions he visited the mill, pleading with his wife to come home. He told her people were making ugly contemptuous remarks about the whole set-up. He also took his complaints to Mrs. Smith who informed him the girl was free to leave if she wished, but she would not be forced from the mill. He must have made himself really objectionable because there was a run-in with Harold, and Mr. Smith stepped in, telling Bradley to stay away from their place. Bradley so persisted in his attempts to persuade Edith to return that finally she went to the police station, where she had an interview with Inspector Anderson in the hope that the authorities could stop her husband from "pestering" her. This put Anderson in a tough spot.

The arrangement at the mill might well offend the social conventions of the time. It might even constitute grounds for divorce, but there was no criminal offence involved. Moreover, the right of a husband to meet and talk with his wife could hardly be ignored. Anderson, with his considerable experience, recognized the sensitive nature of the Smith-Bradley affair. Talking to Andy years later I had the impression he expected trouble, but felt helpless to take any official action to prevent it. However, he did talk to Bradley, and this stopped further visits to the Smith mill until the end of July.

Deprived of the opportunity of seeing his wife and raging with bottled-up jealousy, Bradley now set out to secure local support by putting his own case in a good light and making the Smiths look as black as possible. He asked his employer, J.D. Levesque, if he could borrow his gun, as he feared for his safety when he visited his wife at the mill. Levesque pooh-poohed the request and remarked that "A man shouldn't need a gun to get his wife back to her home."

In small towns, the barber shop is often the focal point for the exchange of information and gossip. With this in mind, Bradley began hanging around Fred Blair's barber shop, located in the building where he lived. He made a point of keeping the barber up-to-date on what was going on. He usually managed to be there when Blair had customers and it wouldn't take long for the outraged husband's complaints to be common knowledge. He accused Harold Smith of kidnapping Edith and holding her prisoner at the Smith home and mill. He graphically described the assaults made upon him by young Smith when he had gone out to see his wife and showed bruises which he claimed were the result.

Next he sat down and wrote a lengthy and detailed account of the whole affair, giving copies to a number of local citizens, including Blair, Mr. Levesque, and a man called Tom Rorke, who was known to have some connection with the court. Rorke served as court reporter later on at Bradley's preliminary hearing, taking down and transcribing witnesses' statements. Rorke was also a witness at the final trial and he recalled his conversation with Bradley when he was given a copy of the latter's bill of complaints, saying in part, "I was sure that Bradley wanted to make certain Harold Smith got a copy." In fact, Rorke made a special trip out to the Smith home to put a copy in young Smith's hands. Harold reacted strongly. "I've got the damn letter already," he raged, "and you can tell Bradley from me that if he comes out here again I'm going to kick him off the place and break him in two."

At the subsequent trial it was part of the Crown's case that Ralph Bradley had by that time made up his mind to kill Harold Smith. This is something only Bradley would know. If he had decided to do so, he was certainly making all the right moves to establish a first-rate working defence.

In murder trials it is fundamental to prove premeditation. No one in possession of normal mental health will make a public declaration of an intent to kill (except in the best international terrorist circles). Thus, in preparing a capital case the Crown will attempt to introduce evidence either directly or by circumstantial means to indicate the accused formed the intent before the deed. Some of the hard facts outlined in this story did not become known until after the final chapter in the case had been written in the jury trial. Looking back on the case some seventy years after the event, a dispassionate analysis does create the strong suspicion that Ralph Bradley formed an intent to kill Harold Smith well before the action was taken. For example, in most cases of deliberate homicide the choice of weapon is critical. Although Bradley was from the western United States where the right to carry a gun was considered an honorable tradition, his employer had already turned down his request to borrow a gun. Public awareness of Bradley's situation would also probably have ruled out the prospect of getting a gun from anyone else in town. So, in late July we find Bradley journeying by boat from Peace River up the Smoky River to catch the train from Watino to Edmonton. There he bought a .38 pistol and box of cartridges. He returned by the next train on Friday, July 23. A man called Dan McCurdy, an acquaintance, also boarded the train at the Calder station and the two met several times during the long, hot trip to Watino. Bradley had no food and very little money, and McCurdy shared the lunch he had brought with him.

The train pulled into the end of steel around 9:00 a.m. the next day. Bradley and McCurdy detrained together, walking down to the passenger boat landing for the last stage of their return trip to Peace River. Two boats provided passenger service down the little river, then, as now, a twisted and tortuous ribbon of white water. Ralph Bradley had made arrangements on his trip out to travel back on the launch, *Beaver,* and had paid his return fare; however, the boat had already left, so he hiked over to see Alfred Hobbs, who operated the other craft, *Lily of the Lake.* As Bradley had only $1.60, not enough even for a one-way ticket, he asked McCurdy to take his other ticket, collect the rebate from the *Beaver*'s operator and give the cash to Hobbs. Hobbs was willing to accept this arrangement after Ralph told him it was necessary he get back to town without delay.

The launch made the voyage down the swiftly-running river in a little over two-and-one-half hours, then pulled out of the Smoky into the quieter waters of the Peace River at a point where the town was visible in the near distance. Bradley pleaded with Hobbs to allow him off at the regular ferry landing, saying it was important he get over to West Peace River as soon as possible, but because of the large number of passengers and the amount of freight, Hobbs decided to land further downstream at the Hudson's Bay dock. It was safer.

Bradley left the boat about 1:30 p.m. He walked back to the ferry landing, crossed to the west side, and without stopping for rest or food, headed straight up the hill road leading to the Smith place. Reaching his destination shortly after 4:00 p.m., he stayed clear of the house, calling for his wife to come out. She finally came to the door and walked over to talk with him. He took hold of her arm, saying, "I've come to get you."

Edith, pulling away said, "Don't touch me! I hate you. You've ruined my whole life and I just don't want to have anything more to do with you!"

"Where is Harold Smith? Is he in the house?"

"No."

"Where is he."

"I'm not sure. In town I guess."

Significantly, there were no threats or abuse to the girl. All too often in cases like this, where feelings run high and reason is in short supply, it is the wife who is killed or beaten on the principle that "if I can't have her, then nobody can." Obviously this was not Ralph Bradley's thinking. He wanted Edith back, but he had not really expected his wife to return with him or he would have brought a team-and-buggy to convey her and her belongings to town. He was simply going through the ritual of asking her one more time before he went off to deal with Harold Smith.

In looking through the dusty old records of the Bradley case and viewing the entire picture from a distance of over seventy years, it appears almost as if Bradley's actions were based on sound advice from a competent criminal lawyer. An effective defence for a charge of murder would include his status as the wronged husband, the detailed written account circulated among people from whom a jury would be selected and the charge that Smith had physically attacked and threatened him. This is all stuff a defence counsel could use to piece together a powerful address to a jury. However, there is nothing to indicate Bradley had sought advice from a criminal lawyer before undertaking this scenario; but there is one pertinent fact not known to the authorities at the time and that appears nowhere on the record. Yet it is most important.

Ralph Bradley had already killed a man!

I had this information from Charlie Roberts and it was confirmed years later by another old-timer. Circumstances surrounding the earlier shooting are vague and I have not been able to corroborate them. I was told only that the shooting took place in the United States and that Bradley had been acquitted on a plea of self-defence. Therefore, perhaps he knew from that experience the requirements of a good defence. Charlie Roberts, who acted for Bradley at his preliminary hearing, was positive no one in Peace River was aware of the earlier murder charge at the time. It was only after the trial was over that Roberts himself learned of it.

Now let us rejoin Ralph Bradley, relentlessly moving towards the final phase of his plan to recover possession of his wife.

From the ferry landing at the west side of the river a path led a few hundred feet through a level stretch and then upwards to the top of a steep cliff where it wound through another large level area known as "the Jack Pines" because of the thick cover of these trees. After about a mile, the road then swung into the hills until it reached the plateau at the crest and then wandered through the homestead area known as '84' where it touched the Smith's place.

Down in the Jack Pines the road forked, with one branch, the shortest, wide enough only for foot passengers or horseback riders going directly to the cliff above West Peace River. The other route, longer and more circuitous, was for buggies and wagons.

On his return trip to town Bradley met two acquaintances. At first he was overtaken by Archie McIntosh about two miles from West Peace River. The two exchanged a few words when Bradley told the other man he was tired and thirsty and wanted to know if McIntosh had seen Harold Smith. Bradley then carried on toward town and McIntosh stayed behind to gather berries. He later caught a ride with a lumber wagon going to Peace River, but got off before he reached the cliff. After he had left the wagon and was walking along the trail McIntosh saw the body of young Harold Smith sprawled just off the pathway.

Shortly after parting from McIntosh, Bradley met Charles Riehl, who was riding horseback. Bradley hailed him to say he was played out, so Riehl took him up on the horse. This was a little after 5:30. The two men rode double either to the fork of the trail or a spot slightly before that point, when Bradley asked to be let off.

Riehl was a little surprised that the weary Bradley elected to walk the rest of the way to town particularly as he chose the longer, winding wagon trail.

Riehl continued on and just after the two trails came together at the top of the cliff, he met a wagon driven by Harold Smith, and his father. This was just before six o'clock, but in late July, with the long northern summer days, it would still be broad daylight. A few minutes later, the Smiths were well into the Jack Pines with their rig. Harold, the driver, was sitting on the left side of the wagon with the reins and a buggy whip in his hand. According to Mr. Smith's account, they suddenly saw a man advancing on foot toward them along the trail on the left of the vehicle as it approached. Startled, the older man looked up, saying "That's Bradley coming at us." Harold did not reply, nor did Bradley say anything.

Mr. W.E. Smith's account of what happened, as given to the police and repeated in his evidence in court, was that just as the rig drew opposite Ralph Bradley, the latter reached into his pocket with his right hand. Recalling he had earlier attempted to borrow a gun from J.D. Levesque and fearful he might be armed now, the father rose from his seat in attempt to jump out and stop him. But in his haste and anxiety he tripped over the reins and buggy whip, caught his knee on a bolt in the dashboard, and fell across Harold, landing heavily on the ground, face down. He recollected that as he fell, his son brought the team to a stop and stood up, but he too lost his balance and crashed to earth just in front of Bradley.

Harold was scrambling to his feet when Bradley shot at him twice with a pistol. The younger Smith began to move toward Bradley, who shot again. This time Harold fell. In fear and anger the father had got up off the ground to go for Bradley, who threatened him with the gun saying, "Don't, or I'll get you too." So Mr. Smith dropped down again. Then, as Harold lay motionless, Ralph Bradley walked up to him and deliberately fired two more shots into his body, after which he cooly turned and went toward town, without uttering another word.

According to W.E. Smith, the entire encounter lasted only a few minutes and nothing was said other than the threat from Bradley to stay put or be shot. The post-mortem examination of Harold Smith revealed four bullet wounds in the upper body, two of which would have caused death, and their location and direction were consistent with their having been fired point-blank into Harold Smith as he lay on the ground.

When Bradley surrendered himself, it was found that three of the five pistol chambers were empty and two were loaded. This means that after killing Harold, he had walked along the trail for a short distance, then calmly paused and partially reloaded his gun, possibly as a defence against the older Smith. Two empty shells were, in fact, found about fifty yards down the trail from where the killing took place.

Bradley did not give evidence at the preliminary hearing, being wisely counselled by his solicitor to reserve his defence. But he was a witness on his own behalf at the jury trial when he gave his version of the shooting. He swore he saw the rig approaching and, just as it began to pass him, the Smiths leapt out, bent on attack. He did admit that their only weapon was a buggy whip. As they advanced, Bradley said, he pulled out his pistol and fired one warning shot into the air. Harold did not stop and, as he came closer, he shot four times in self defence.

After reloading his gun Bradley had walked to West Peace River, to the barber shop, in the same building where he lived. There, according to Fred Blair, the barber, Bradley told his story in a calm and collected manner, beginning with the words, "Well, I done it."

"Done what? What did you do?"

"Well, I've shot him."

"Who?"

"Harold."

"Where did you shoot him?"

"In the Jack Pine flats. I will give myself up to you if you will take me over to the police."

"All right. But first give me the gun and ammunition."

Whereupon the two went immediately to the ferry landing, only to see the ferry had just left. Blair hailed the operator, hoping to persuade him to return but the ferry kept moving. They saw a motor launch just pulling into the landing and called to the boatman, who took them aboard and ferried them to the police station on the east side of the river.

According to Blair and other witnesses, from the time Bradley appeared at the barber shop until he was locked up, he remained composed and unemotional. He greeted by name the people he met, shook hands, and made normal conversation with them, even with the men at the police station. When Bradley and Blair arrived there they found Inspector Anderson and a constable had just rushed down to the ferry landing after receiving a telephone call from W.E. Smith. Smith had waited in the Jack Pines until he felt it was safe to leave, then he galloped his team to the ferry, crossed over, and at once telephoned the authorities.

Bradley and Blair stayed in the office until Inspector Anderson returned, when Blair turned over the pistol and ammunition. Bradley was then formally arrested, given the statutory warning, and placed in a cell.

At the preliminary hearing, held in Peace River, July 31, 1915, just a week after the tragedy, Bradley exercised his right not to make any statement. The only witness who spoke about the actual shooting was W.E. Smith whose testimony, in general, followed the story outlined earlier. However others, including those people who had met and talked with Bradley July 24, corroborated various phases of the evidence. Edith Bradley was also a witness. She told about the days of her meeting and early relationship with Bradley, and carried her testimony forward in detail to the day of the shooting. What she said was not very helpful to Bradley.

It is significant that Charlie Roberts, who appeared for Bradley at the preliminary inquiry, made no objection to the girl being brought forward as a witness. I believe this was because those closely related to the proceedings felt the marriage was not valid. In any event, it was an astute move on Roberts's behalf to allow her to tell her story. Her testimony made for a better cross-examination later at the trial. Certainly, at the beginning of the criminal proceedings, Bradley needed all the help he could get.

The shock of the killing and the details which did leak out had turned sympathy against Bradley, although as his jury trial date came closer, public opinion began to change. It is a fascinating study in how the residents of a close-knit, small town may change their thinking in such a short time. Amazingly, it was only 36 days from the time Harold Smith lay lifeless in the Jack Pines that the man who had shot him faced a judge and jury. What a remarkable contrast to the present day, when months and often years separate the crime and the ultimate judicial decision.

Local papers in rural areas usually mirror the trend of thought in the community and the Peace River paper when first reporting the Smith killing hadn't the slightest hesitation in coming to an immediate judgment.

"MURDER ON SATURDAY JULY 24th" its headline shouted and in the following story Harold Smith was referred to as "a well-known and popular young man." The report went on to say, "Bradley drew his revolver and began firing rapidly and with deadly aim, four bullets striking the victim." Even more damaging to Bradley was a direct quote attributed to him just after his arrest: "When asked if he had shot the father too, he replied, *No, I am glad I did not have to injure him as it was not him I was after.*"

The next edition of the weekly paper reported the preliminary inquiry and had this to say about Edith Bradley and her appearance as a witness: "She, considered the indirect cause of the shooting, expressed no sympathy for her husband."

Yet when the supreme court jury trial was held one month later, it was fully reported, and the reporter painted an entirely different picture, which I will deal with later.

But at the start the only friend Bradley seemed to have, according to the paper, was Mrs. Cook, his wife's mother. She expressed "deepest sympathy for the young man and assured him of her best endeavors on his behalf." I have a feeling she paid for lawyers for the penniless Ralph Bradley.

The purpose of a preliminary inquiry is to determine if there is enough evidence to send the accused to trial at a higher court. In other words, it is to establish a prima facie case. In the Bradley case there was no problem doing this and he was duly committed for trial without bail to the next court of competent jurisdiction at Peace River, i.e., the next sitting of a supreme court with jury. He was sent to Fort Saskatchewan near Edmonton to await the event.

Turning over the police files and government documents, I found that immediately after the inquiry Edith Bradley took off. By then she had probably had enough of Peace River and excitement. Possibly she thought that having been in one courthouse and given her sworn testimony she was all through with the affair. But it was not as easy as that. The RNWMP caught up with her in Edmonton, warned her not to leave the jurisdiction and arranged accommodation for her until the supreme court trial. This was laid on for August 30th, at which time the department of the attorney general brought her back to Peace River and paid her fare. I saw in the documents a receipt for $20 for the cost of a buggy and driver from the end of steel at Reno down to Peace River. Some of her family accompanied her.

E.B. Cogswell, K.C., was sent from Edmonton as the chief prosecutor, while the Hon. A.G. McKay, K.C., a member of the Alberta Legislative Assembly and a well-known counsel, travelled up on the same train to take charge of the defence. Cogswell, a senior member of the attorney general's staff and later the chief Crown prosecutor at Edmonton, was a slight man who walked with a limp. He had a strong voice and could look very fierce when required to deal with an evasive witness. In fact, he was an ideal prosecutor for our criminal justice system. He was still around when I was a law student and sat in with my father on some of his defences. So I did get to know something of Mr. Cogswell. He was always straightforward and fair in his approach to a trial when representing the Crown. I suppose like most people he liked to win, but he never thought that was his primary function. He never sought to take undue advantage or obtain a conviction by dubious methods and he never refused to bring out the whole truth. His attitude was that he had a solemn duty to lay all the facts before the judge and the jury and let the chips fall where they may. McKay, the defence counsel, was a big burly man. Colorful, emotional, with a commanding presence and a well-tuned voice, he had a grand way with a jury.

Mr. Justice Beck was the trial judge. A warm and very human personality, he was later to serve with distinction for many years as a member of the Alberta appellate division of the supreme court where he was often a dissenter in his judgments, which were likely to extend the law to consider human needs.

The law enforcement authorities engaged in the conduct of Bradley's prosecution had good reason to believe they could secure a conviction for murder; at the very least they thought that Ralph Bradley would be lucky to get away with a verdict of manslaughter and a long sentence. His case was one of a large class with certain common characteristics, where a plea of self-defence is vigorously advanced on behalf of someone charged with murder. Very frequently an astute counsel for the accused will attempt to smuggle in, under the cloak of such a plea, facts which are strictly irrelevant, but which may be linked to other material and can well be calculated to influence a jury. If insanity is not being put forward to further confuse a jury, there are three options as to the kind of verdict that can be brought in: Guilty of murder; guilty of manslaughter; not guilty. Fundamentally, one may use force to defend oneself against an attack. The fine point of law here is that the degree of force used to repel an attack in self-defence must be related to the type and amount of force used by the attacker.

This principle might seem simple enough to legal Monday morning quarterbacks. Yet on this issue thousands of pages have been written and countless learned judgments have been handed down by courts and judges at every level. Having been involved in many of these cases and witnessed others, I can only say it is impossible to say for certain what a verdict will be before the foreman of a jury rises to face the accused and delivers the verdict.

Examining the Bradley matter from this late perspective and considering the law and its strict application, there had to be a strong leaning towards a murder conviction. Giving the highest value to Bradley's story, the kind and amount of force he was threatened with, the buggy whip, it did not justify the fire power with which he responded. And then there were so many incidents, minor by themselves but which taken together, seemed to point to premeditation, the establishment of an intent to do Harold Smith in.

But that was the law. In the court we move to the beat of a different drum; the law is but one element. The judge tells the jury he is there to advise them of the law, but they, the jury, those six good men and true have the final word. It is for them to assess the evidence and observe the demeanor of the witnesses and having filtered what has been said and presented through its collective mind, reach a verdict.

Finally, this was the north. It was a society and a time geared to the principle of male domination, even to a husband's proprietary interest in his wife. It was, after all, just a generation after the Victorian era when the conventions of the law, not merely allowed, but in some instances, legalized this attitude.

Trial proceedings are transcribed whenever an appeal is taken from the judgment. In the days when the death penalty existed and an accused was sentenced to be hanged, a copy of the proceedings at the trial was made available to the federal cabinet. Before execution the Governor General exercised one of the few remaining prerogatives of the Crown and decided whether to grant clemency and commute the sentence or refuse to interfere. The executive council, as constitutional adviser to His Excellency, had studied each case and offered advice after all other avenues of appeal were eliminated or abandoned. Diefenbaker, as a lawyer, had handled a number of capital defences and was very much aware of what was involved. He told me once that as Prime Minister, he felt these decisions were amongst the most difficult the cabinet had to work out.

My information about Bradley's trial has been taken from such government papers, as well as documents from police files and eyewitness accounts.

The evidence at the supreme court jury trial followed pretty faithfully that given at the preliminary inquiry, except for Bradley's entering the witness box to give evidence on his own behalf and one or two minor witnesses not being called for the Crown.

There was one major difference. That was the cross examination of Crown witnesses by McKay.

A wise defence counsel utilizes the earlier inquiry to carefully assess and evaluate the evidence, study the witnesses to determine how they will react to a well-planned and vigorous cross examination, and look for weaknesses in the structure of the prosecution's case. This does not mean that a witness at the preliminary is not probed. But usually it is deemed sensible not to indicate too fully the probable nature of the defence and how it will be developed at the final trial, so the accused can retain all his options.

Now this is the way things go in real life, unlike television court dramas such as the Perry Mason series, where supernaturally brilliant lawyers astound the spectators, the court, the district attorney, and, most importantly, the television audience, by compelling the real murderer to stand up and admit his guilt during the preliminary hearing.

All the stops, however, are pulled out when the case is actually before the jury. In the Bradley case, McKay's handling of the witnesses and, in particular, his cross-examination, was brilliant. With many of the Crown witnesses, he adopted a soft and silky approach, knowing that, in the main, those not related to the police or Crown authorities would be inclined to look with sympathy upon Bradley and there would be no point in antagonizing them. As they were not defence witnesses he also had more latitude in his questioning. Much of what these people had to say was slanted in favor of the accused. Only while questioning W.E. Smith did McKay thunder and challenge.

In turn, Bradley was subjected to a powerful cross-examination by Cogswell. He had difficulty reconciling some of his statements and explaining certain of his actions, but he did not lose his composure. When he finally emerged from the ordeal he was battered and bruised, but not broken.

During the final summing-up by counsel, McKay made a powerful and moving address. He had so much material to draw upon—the stealing of the wife; the threats to Bradley; the difference in size and strength of the men; the fact that Harold had his father to back him up; the poor little man against the successful, and unpopular family. McKay told them all the things they wanted to hear: that the north did not look kindly on wife stealing; that no man need sit idly by and allow his woman to be taken from him; that the Smiths had so abused and threatened Bradley, he required a pistol to defend himself; that he so feared these big powerful men upon seeing them dismount from the vehicle with the intent to batter, and possibly kill him, he shot only to defend himself. Scorning the middle course of asking for a verdict of manslaughter, McKay then stood tall before the jury and demanded a complete acquittal.

McKay was speaking to the already converted, and his words served only to confirm their thinking. I am certain when he was finished anything the Crown prosecutor had to say fell on deaf ears.

The final words spoken were by Mr. Justice Beck. He delivered the case and the fate of the accused into the hands of the jury, who had no doubt in their minds that McKay had chosen well to demand they either find the accused guilty of murder or set him free.

The jury retired for only a period of fifteen minutes—to satisfy the demands of politeness—before returning with the verdict: "NOT GUILTY!" Then, after the presiding justice had called on

Bradley to rise and told him he was free to go, there occurred a scene not often witnessed in Canadian courts. Applause and wild cheering filled the air as the spectators in the crowded theatre where the proceedings had taken place put Bradley on their shoulders and surged from the building to join the people waiting outside.

Bradley was the man of the hour, the popular hero of the day. The celebrations spilled across the town and even into West Peace River.

Understandably the police were not happy about the verdict. Corporal A.C. Hatfield of the force's Peace River detachment, who reported the proceedings, had some writing ability. In his concluding summary of the case of Rex vs. Bradley, he makes this cryptic observation, "The verdict appeared to be very popular with certain classes!" No doubt Bradley was not their idea of a popular civic hero. However, the last sentence of Hatfield's report made me really sit up. "Bradley with his wife and party left immediately after the trial for Nebraska USA."

Bradley with his wife?

So, after the ordeal of the trial with all its baggage of hate and violence, they returned to the United States as man and wife.

Why?

What persuaded this girl, who had said privately and publicly that Ralph Bradley had ruined her life, that she did not love him, and wanted nothing more to do with him, to go back to him? She was with members of her family who had come north to be with her during the trial, so she did have a choice. The most probable reason is that she was young and impressionable. She had been an actor, as well as a fascinated spectator, throughout the proceedings. She had watched wide-eyed the dramatic end of the case, when Bradley, declared by the law to be not guilty of murder had been set free, then immediately taken up and made the man of the moment by a shouting cheering mob.

All these events must have mesmerized her, made him a heroic figure, and pushed her back into his arms. There are no records, nothing at all to show what took place in the lives of these two after they left the north. Did they remarry? Did Bradley get his hands on her money? Did they continue to stay together? We have the chronicle of their first turbulent year together and then they disappear from sight.

After I had written this story I was able to read the account of the trial in Peace River as reported in the Peace River Record of Thursday September 2, 1915, which was provided for me by the kindness of the editor Pear Muir of the current *Peace River Record Gazette* which still circulates in the district.

Whoever wrote the report for the paper shows an obvious bias for Bradley and against the Smiths, indicating the change in the public mood since the earlier hearing. Here are excerpts from the news story on the front page of the *Peace River Record Gazette* Thursday, September 2, 1915.

"NOT GUILTY"
is Verdict of Jury
in Bradley Trial.
Verdict is greeted by tremendous burst of applause.
Wife returns with acquitted husband to former home
in Denver Colorado.

"When on Tuesday afternoon, shortly before four o'clock, T.A. Brick, foreman of the jury, announced to a hushed court Ralph W. Bradley was not guilty of the murder of young Harold Smith and thus brought to a dramatic conclusion a case that has excited the most intense local interest for several weeks, pandemonium broke loose in the crowded building. Men and women alike cheered themselves hoarse, and even the court orderly after once attempting to restore order, decided that the only thing to do was to allow the general jubilation to have full sway.

Hon. A.G. Mackay, whose able defence had a good deal to do with the final result, said afterwards that in all his twenty-two years experience at the bar he had never seen such a striking display of popular feeling.

But, apart from the excitement caused by the verdict, the incident during the final scenes that appealed most to the popular imagination was the reconciliation between the young girl-wife and heiress, Mrs. Bradley, and her husband. No sooner had the jury given their decision than Mrs. Bradley, radiant with joy, stepped up to him, threw her arms around his neck, and kissed him unrestrainedly, the while everybody in court looked on delightedly. The most brilliant novelist could not have given a plot a happier ending.

One of the features of the case was the severe castigation of W.E. Smith and his wife by Mr. McKay, who said he had never heard of a more "bold faced, barefaced, immoral breach of the law" than by them. Mr. McKay also hinted that the Smiths were actuated in influencing Mrs. Bradley by the fact that she was an heiress to the sum of about forty thousand dollars, to come into her full right in November next and added that if she had been worth only forty cents this difficulty would not have occurred. These remarks brought cheers from the crowded court room, until the judge finally was obliged to state that if there were any more of these demonstrations, he would have to clear the court, adding that the case would have to be tried by the jury not by the audience. His Lordship referred to the Smiths in his charge and said he could not find words that would sufficiently condemn their actions.

The facts of the case are too well known locally to need recapitulation. There was a stir in court, however, when Bradley himself was put in the box, and every eye was turned towards him as he tearfully related his harrowing experiences. He told of the happiness of himself and his wife until Harold Smith appeared on the scene; their gradual estrangement and finally their separation, when she exclaimed "Ralph don't you dare touch me. I hate you, you have ruined my life."

For the greater part of the time, Bradley told his story without the slightest prompting from Mr. McKay. Soon after they had become acquainted with Harold Smith, he said his wife put her hands on his shoulders, looked in his eyes, and said, "Ralph, help me to be faithful to you." He wanted to know what she meant, but she could not tell him. Things moved swiftly after she stayed all one night at the Smith home. "Edith," he asked, "what are we going to do?" and she replied "Ralph, I don't love you" and added that she was homesick and unhappy.

Meeting Harold Smith, shortly afterwards, Bradley wanted to know whether his wife was in a similar mental condition at the Smith home, and young Smith replied "She was as happy as could be, having one hell of a time."

She again returned to the Smiths. "I went to fetch her back" said Bradley. "She told me she did not love me any more, and she had made up her mind to leave me. She said Harold was not to blame, but that she thought it a crime to live with a man she did not love—"

Bradley said he asked Harold, if he could stay all night, and Harold replied "There's no room here for you." Bradley accused Smith of "playing the dirtiest doggiest trick ever done by one man to another."

During another trip to the Smith home Bradley found his wife arm in arm with Harold. "Boy" she told Bradley "I like you but I don't love you. Don't have any hopes. I can't come back. Good bye" and she kissed him farewell. That was the time when Harold defiantly exclaimed "people will talk, but what do we care?"

Bradley endeavored to reason with Harold and explained that he could not legally do anything unless he brought a charge of adultery. "By God, then, that's what you will have to do."

"I accused him" said Bradley "of stealing her from me, and he cursed me, grabbed me by the arm and struck me on the head, and knocked me flat on the ground. 'The next time' he said 'you will get worse.'"

Hon. A.G. McKay made one of his characteristically eloquent addresses to the jury "Provocation and self defence" was the burden of his plea, and he made the most of it. Harold Smith he termed "a freebooter in the affections of the Bradley family" and referring to the elder Smith, said a man who would warn the husband away and keep the wife as he did was lost to all sense of moral responsibility. "I would not like to advise lawlessness" said Mr. McKay "but if the whole Smith family had to be carried out of the house feet foremost, I, if I had been in Bradley's place, would have brought my wife away with me."

After the verdict had been given, and some degree of order had been restored Mr. Justice Beck said the verdict in this particular case must not be construed to mean that lynch law and wanton killing in cold blood and the taking of the law into one's own hands were permissible in Canada, as offenders in this regard would be dealt with according to the full rigors of the law."

After reading this rather prosy piece in a style common to the period, I turned the old paper to the editorial page to see what view the editor might have taken of the case.

What I found was a satiric piece written by some cynical soul:

"The refusal of Canadian Courts to consider the unwritten law as a justification for murder leaves Canadians free to administer to a wrongdoer the same punishment as an Englishman, who finding a man with his wife in the bedroom, was asked what he said or did about it. 'What did I say to him, why, nothing. I hadn't been introduced to the fellow! But I got even with him— on the way out of my house I saw he had left his gold-plated cane so I took it and broke the cane to pieces.'"

CHAPTER THREE

Tragedy at Golden Meadow

IT WAS A COLD DECEMBER MORNING IN 1937 WITH A bitter wind whistling down Main Street and snow drifting up over the sidewalks. I had just started to glance through my mail at the office when the telephone rang. It was an old friend, Corporal Harry Lowes calling from the Peace River RCMP subdivision headquarters.

"Ged, there's a man down here who's pretty anxious to talk to you."

"Someone I know?"

"Says he's never met you. His name is Harvey Thompson, and he's from the Golden Meadow country south of Whitelaw. He's charged with—"

"I know," I interrupted, "he's charged with murdering his wife."

In truth the case had received wide coverage in the northern press as well as the Edmonton media. The charred remains of a woman had been found in a burned-out house on the Thompson farm. The woman had been identified tentatively as Mrs. Bertha Thompson and her husband, Harvey, was being held in custody. One extraordinary aspect of the case was that some domestic pets—two cats and three dogs—had also been killed with a heavy instrument. Their bodies were found outside the burned dwelling house close by the pumphouse.

I was well acquainted with the Golden Meadow district, a beautiful, fertile farming countryside, sloping gently from the north towards the banks of the Peace river. It was inhabited by fine, solid citizens, good farmers and excellent neighbors, not the kind of people associated with domestic violence. Yet only a few weeks earlier I had been retained to act for a Mrs. Jenny Robertson, who lived a few miles north of Golden Meadow and who was now in jail charged with the murder of her husband. So here were two domestic tragedies within a space of three months in this peaceful farming community.

"Thanks, Harry," I said, "tell Mr. Thompson I'll be there as soon as I can, and tell him I don't like my clients to talk to policemen."

This was something of a joke between Harry Lowes and me; there was a chuckle on the other end of the line. I could almost see Harry's grin. As well as representing the Crown at preliminary hearings, Harry often conducted prosecutions in magistrate's court. Harry replied, "This fellow didn't need encouragement. He was willing and happy to talk. Seriously, Ged, I think you'll be happy Mr. Thompson told us his story, and I don't think you'll find it too bad."

"We'll wait and see," I answered. Many were the tangles Lowes and I had over the thorny question of admitting into evidence statements given by accused persons to police before they had the benefit of advice from a lawyer.

"Say, Harry, my car is frozen-up at home in this 30°-below stuff. Will you have a police car going from the town detachment to the barracks in the next hour or so?"

"Sure," Harry said cheerfully, "I'll tell the boys from the detachment office to give you a ring before they head this way."

Within the hour, I found myself sitting across a small table from Thompson in the little whitewashed cell below the subdivision offices. I took an instinctive liking to the man. In my work as a criminal lawyer I did not find many of the characters I met congenial, but it was not my job to make social contacts. I gave those who asked for my help the best defence the law and the rules of my profession would permit. A plan of strategy for defence has to be based on something more than a first reaction to a client. Nevertheless, I felt a sympathy for Thompson. He appeared to be a shy and diffident person. Although of average height, he seemed shorter. His head and shoulders were bent as if he anticipated physical or verbal abuse. His face was lined and ruddy and his red hair thatched with gray. I judged him to be in his early to middle fifties. He had a soft, easy voice and he appeared to be a better listener than a talker—hardly the stuff from which wife-murderers, let alone killers of household pets, are made. Yet I know appearances are deceptive. Circumstances can push people to violent acts, far out of character. Thompson began to speak before I had time to take my pad and pen from my briefcase.

"I guess the big corporal (Lowes was a tall and well set-up man) said I wanted to see you. They tell me I'm in quite a mess." His voice turned forlorn, "But I know you'll do your best to help me. You had a good name from the Grovers, my neighbors in Golden Meadows, and the police here speak pretty well of you."

Then his reserve fell away. His voice turned strong and passionate as the words gushed out. It was, in fact, the only time I heard him talk this way.

"You know, Mr. Baldwin, that woman made the last eight or ten years of my life pure hell. I left her not so long ago and went out to British Columbia and had a good job. I shouldn't ever have come back. But they wrote me and said she really needed me and things would be much better if I came back to the Peace, and they were sure we could make a go at the farm. I was crazy enough to do what they asked, and now look where I am."

He put his head down on the table and when he raised it, tears were running down his cheeks. I waited a few minutes until he'd calmed down before I spoke, "Just a couple of questions, Mr. Thompson. Were you responsible for your wife's death? And have you made any statements to the police?"

"Yes, sir, God help me, I did kill her. It was the first time I'd ever really struck her, and I'm telling you the truth, just like I told the police. But after she threw the hot food in my face, I just couldn't hold it back. That's when it started. Later, in the night, when I woke up and saw her creeping up on me with a knife in her hand, I really lost control and picked up that chair and . . ."

"I'm sorry to interrupt, Mr. Thompson, but maybe you'd better start at the beginning. Take it slow and easy, we have plenty of time."

He stopped, thought, then went back to the early days of his marriage just after he had come from the United States to enlist in the Canadian army in the First World War. Occasionally he jumped to the present and once or twice he talked of the years before his marriage, including the period he had served with the American peacetime armed forces. Although he never said so, it was apparent his marriage was a mistake from the start. There had been only a few days courtship before the marriage had taken place in eastern Canada. There was a short honeymoon before he had been shipped overseas to France. It was a familiar pattern I was to note in my experience with domestic problems of marriages from both wars—a quick marriage, followed by a separation, and, afterwards, the realization it was all a mistake. At the end of the Second World War, divorce had become an acceptable fact of our social fabric. Many of the ill-starred marriages of that period were later sensibly ended by dissolution. Divorce was not as simple or acceptable for people who had come through the First World War. Quite a few of these couples came north, hoping that a fresh start in the new and adventurous atmosphere of the Peace River country would prove a cure for their domestic problems. The Thompson case was one of those. Although Thompson did his best to put it all together during the several hours of our first interview, his story was disconnected and incoherent.

I realized he would not be a good witness. I had a feeling he was truthful, but his jerky presentation and eagerness to please could make him a sitting duck for a tough, ruthless cross-examination. This is always a critical question for a defence counsel. Do you put your client on the stand? If an accused does not testify, there will be no comment from the prosecution or the bench. The jury, however, is not always sophisticated enough to understand this fine point. It is sometimes better to put a poor witness in the box than to have the jury wondering, "Why doesn't he want to tell his story?"

Early in my career at the bar I read the biography of the famous English defence counsel, Sir Edward Marshall Hall. His approach to this knotty problem was to explain the law and issues at stake to an accused client, then have the latter write his or her decision about giving evidence on a piece of paper—"I wish to give evidence" or "I do not wish to give evidence."

While doing research for this chapter I came upon a document in the file of the attorney general which only became known to me during the course of the case. It was a report by the superintendent of the government mental institute to which Thompson had been sent while near Edmonton awaiting trial.

It had been obvious to me from the start that insanity was not a plea which could be advanced. The Crown, however, thought I might do so and arranged for an examination of Thompson by Dr. McAlister, the superintendent of the government mental institute near Edmonton. Reading the report later, I found it basically consistent with the story mumbled to me by that sad little man on that cold December morning in the basement cell of police headquarters. It had the pathos embedded in the lives of so many people, who, in the beginning, did not seem to be the material from which would erupt such violent tragedy.

Psychiatric Report

Re: Harvey L. Thompson
Peace River, Alta.

"Thompson was born in Iowa, September 28, 1886. He states there are no serious childhood illnesses. He finished the eighth grade at 18 years. The latter years he attended school during winter time only. No school problems. States he was rather reserved and aloof up until 15 years of age. "Was bashful." Never cared much for parties. During youth was not interested in very much except farming work. Mixed freely with men but was rather shy with opposite sex. Had extra-marital experiences but not before he was 21 years of age, after he had left home for the first time. He states his habits were moderate. Drank moderately and did not use tobacco until 1917. He served in the United States marines in 1915 and developed Malaria in Philippines. Married in April 1918, Kingston, Ont. He had known his wife less than a month. She was a widow and states she lost her husband and two children. Wife actually was separated from her husband. She was 39 years of age at the time of her marriage. She had no education. Could not read or write and had no interest in learning. Did not know much about her people. The patient was in the Canadian army at that time and went overseas that spring with the RCHA. He returned to Canada in the spring of 1919 and they both went west to Edmonton. They went to the Peace River and farmed on a half section, receiving government assistance. In the winter of 1919 he was working in a coal mine and returned to the Peace River in 1920. Wife's conduct during this time quite acceptable. Was apparently in good health. Wife was a good cook but couldn't make fancy dishes. Got on well until 1928 when wife became disatisfied and wanted new things, house, car, etc. Prisoner states he went into debt for car and house in order to meet her wishes. But she was still more or less dissatisfied. He states she was always high-tempered and became violent, using profane, obscene language during her outbursts. Home conditions became such that he left her in 1935 and came back and sold out and they went to the coast where he was employed in various jobs. She was dissatisfied there and wanted to return, so came back in the spring of 1937 and went on the farm again. States his wife always imagined she was going to have a baby and she was so convinced that the doctor was called in. He denied pregnancy. Wife said, "Doctor does not know what he is talking about." This was well after the menopause apparently. She also imagined she had all sorts of ills. Kept taking patent medicines and drugs. While at the coast she lost weight and developed an abscess in the hip, but X-ray did not reveal anything at the time. I gather from other data it was T.B. of the spine. Wife was a semi-invalid after coming from the coast. She had to have help. She was very jealous of him and the hired girl. Always very suspicious and very "evil minded." Got so she insulted every woman that came around. Prisoner states that after coming back he was trying to please and pull things together. Wife was not co-operative. In tempers she threw things at him. He never attacked her before the following incident. He prepared the supper on the night of Dec. 3rd. They were both sitting at the table. After some wordy exchanges wife threw a hot potato in his face. He choked her. He assisted her to bed. She went to sleep at the time but the prisoner did not. He kept the light burning. His wife wakened at 3 o'clock and said: "Where is that man who choked me. I will kill him." She jumped up and got a knife from between the cupboard and buffet and came toward him with it. He came toward her and when she attempted to come around the chair he took it and used it as a weapon. When he realized what he had done he decided to end it all. With that in mind he went out to the pump house and while there saw the dogs and cats and feeling he would not like to leave them unprotected, killed them all. He then went back to the house with gasoline. He grabbed a knife but could not kill himself. He left the house and, partly running, came to the nearest village and asked that he be taken in custody.

Family History

Father, dead, aged 63 years, pneumonia. Mother, dead, aged 77. Died of fracture. Two sisters, one dead, aged 55; "Was a Christian Scientist and would not call a doctor."

Physical

Well developed man. Apparently near the age stated (51 years). Examination did not reveal any gross lesion or defect. Special senses quite intact except for visual. Requires glasses for reading.

Mental State

His appearance during the two interviews was that of a person quite calm and collected. He was co-operative and talked in a rational and coherent manner. There was no evidence of anything abnormal in his trend of thought or in the stream of his mental activity. Intellectually I would say he is normal. The contents of talk during the interview did not reveal any mental disorder. No evidence of hallucination. Memory was good; orientation correct. Judgment and reasoning apparently normal. Insight intact. His personality quite well integrated. The emotional tone did not appear abnormal, although he did exhibit considerable distress as a result of the tragedy.

Findings

It is my opinion that this man is not suffering from any form of psychosis. There was apparently considerable accumulated emotional tension on his part as a result of the unreasonable attitude of his wife. This he held in check up to the night of the tragedy when, following her attempt to assault him, he gave way to his emotions with the tragic results."

Dr. McAlister had been engaged in other cases where I was acting for the defence and I had always found him to be methodical and objective in his studies and reports, unlike many of his colleagues who have a tendency to acquire a bias for the side that engages them. One statement leaped from the page:

> There was apparently considerable emotional tension on his part as a result of the unreasonable attitude of his wife. This he held in check up to the night of the tragedy when, following her attempt to assault him, he gave way to his emotions . . .

It confirmed my first impression of the man, later reinforced from other sources. I just did not think he was intellectually capable of faking emotional distress or dogged enough to continue the role during many interviews with me and others. Other important aspects came to light during that first interview.

When I asked Thompson why he went to Whitelaw to give himself up to the police, he told me his first thought when he began the nine-mile walk to town was to catch the early morning train to Edmonton, then try to make it to the United States where he could disappear. "But," he continued, "as I walked in the cold, it came to me that I didn't want to be running and hiding for the rest of my life. I felt remorse for what had taken place. I looked back and saw the smoke from the house. I changed my mind."

I asked him about the macabre killing of the dogs and cats. He hesitated. "Well, Mr. Baldwin, Bertha didn't care all that much for them. She only kept them to spite me. It's not that I didn't like the animals, but she made such a fuss over them and used to let them in the house until it was a mess and had a bad smell. It was beginning to get me down. But I really did feel if they were left they would starve or freeze before anyone found them. So I went to the pumphouse where they were kept at night and killed them with an axe."

It was getting along by then. I gathered my notes and prepared to leave. Just as I reached the door and was about to call the guard, Thompson motioned me to come back.

"I guess I have to tell you something I haven't said to anyone yet. You know I felt Bertha's pulse and there was nothing. I was sure she was dead. So I got the gas, spilled it around, and started the fire. But after I came back from the pumphouse with more gas I heard a noise from her. I knew it was the death rattle as I'd heard it before. It startled me so much, I reached for the axe and hit her with it. By that time the fire was well away, so I shut the door and started off for Whitelaw."

His face was tight and set. I knew he would never be able to wipe the incident from his mind. It was a shocking statement. As I walked out to my taxi, I realized I had a formidable task ahead of me.

The next morning I went carefully over my notes and reviewed my impressions of Thompson. I felt sure that, short of an emergency, he must not be put on the witness stand. His story about using an axe on his wife might not technically make his actions any more or less a murder, but it was sure to have an adverse effect on a jury. The part of Thompson's story which could save his life would have to be heard through the words of others—witnesses called by the defence or the cross-examination of Crown witnesses, or better still from the statement Thompson made to the police just after he was arrested. The prosecution would be compelled to put it forward in order to connect Thompson with the death of his wife. The Crown must show that any statement made by a person placed under arrest is voluntary. The idea is to dispel suspicion that confession is forced by brutality or trickery. With this thought in mind, I got on the telephone to subdivision headquarters and pointed out that because the preliminary hearing was to be brought on immediately, I must be allowed to see Thompson's written statement. There was a discussion at the other end, then the officer came back to the line to say I could have a copy.

The two-page document was a straightforward account of the facts very much along the same lines as Thompson's conversation with me. It set out the events of December 3, 1937, until Thompson arrived in Whitelaw when he had reported his wife's death and asked that the RCMP at Fairview be notified. There were a few additions, not of any consequence, but no mention of his use of an axe on his wife. My immediate reaction was that the statement would provide a good foundation for a plea to reduce the charge of murder to manslaughter. We could avoid the pitfalls and dangers of placing him on the witness stand where he might be badly discredited.

At my third meeting with Thompson I went over the story again, slowly and painstakingly. Using my notes and his statement to the police, I challenged him on the soft points just as if this were a cross-examination. Fundamentally he stayed within the framework of what he had first told me. There was nothing, however, which persuaded me to reverse my decision that it would be too great a risk for him to give testimony on his own behalf. With what Harvey Thompson carried in his mind, court-room scrutiny would be devastating.

The preliminary was set for Peace River in two days' time. It would then adjourn to Whitelaw. I told Thompson I would be with him both days and that we would not put in any sort of formal defence at this stage. I would limit myself to questioning witnesses called by the police and checking the document, photos, and sketches produced. I warned him it was inevitable he would be committed for trial and sent to Fort Saskatchewan to await a supreme court jury sitting. I also told him it was a very good bet he would be examined by a psychiatrist before coming to trial. I said "Harvey, don't worry about it. I know you're ok but let the government figure that we might plead insanity and it will tend to confuse them and scatter their case." I also suggested he give me the names and addresses of neighbors he knew to be friendly and who were aware of the circumstances under which he and his wife lived. I intended to summon them as witnesses if we needed them, and I wanted to add a little more confusion to the prosecution.

The inquiry came on before Magistrate William Stewart with Lowes acting for the Crown. Corporal Walker of the RCMP and Dr. McFadyen, a local medical doctor were Crown witnesses. Both had witnessed the grisly spectacle of Bertha Thompson's burned corpse being removed from the still smoking ruins of the farm dwelling. At Whitelaw a few residents of the district were produced, including a Whitelaw Justice of the Peace named Spotiswoode, to whom Thompson had surrendered, and Mrs. Grover, a neighbor of the Thompsons. The written statement of the accused was also submitted as evidence. I went through the motions of objecting to the production of the statement, knowing that the magistrate would be bound to admit it as an exhibit and once before the court it was on a judicial assembly line and would therefore be available to be read to the jury in the high court. The authorities were of course on the horns of a dilemma —while the statement contained material favorable to the defence, it was the only evidence then available to connect Thompson with the death of his wife—and they had no option but to put forward the document with the best grace they could.

I stole a look at Thompson as the statement was being read in court but he was sitting with his head bowed down and his hands over his eyes, so I was unable to assess his reaction to the story he had given. The statement was admitted over my objection.

As the Crown's case unfolded and the witnesses were questioned, it became increasingly clear that people felt a sympathy for Thompson's plight.

This attitude, if carried over to the supreme court hearing, must to some extent influence the course of that trial. There might be a studied indifference to this sort of thing in the offices of an attorney-general, but we who were in the forward trenches of the judicial system in the north knew it was a very vital element which it was dangerous to ignore. While this case would involve some consideration of the law, it was to a great extent a question of fact. It was the way a jury might be expected to react to the circumstances taking place in the daily lives of ordinary people, circumstances which the average jury could well understand, that would carry the most weight. For this reason, the unseen, sometimes unspoken feeling of a community was a real factor.

The uneasiness I had first experienced about the Harvey Thompson affair began to evaporate and by the end of the inquiry, I felt there was a good prospect that we could have a verdict of manslaughter with a limited term of imprisonment rather than murder with the mandatory death penalty.

After Thompson had been sent outside to Fort Saskatchewan to await trial, I went to Whitelaw and made it my headquarters for several days while I travelled the district and talked to many people, including those neighbors on the list he gave me. I visited over twenty farms, talked to teachers at the local schools, elevator agents to whom he had sold grain, business people he had dealt with, not only in Whitelaw, but in the neighboring communities of Bluesky, Brownvale, and Fairview. I did not find any person who had a bad word for Thompson. Finally I travelled some distance to speak to a girl called Barbara Bast, who had spent six months at the Thompson place working in the house and looking after Bertha. The girl said that Mrs. Thompson's temper and tantrums had been too much for her and that that was why she had to leave. She added that Harvey took a great deal of abuse with remarkable restraint and had tried to make life easier for his wife.

After I left the Bast place I went to see Dr. Matt Matas at Berwyn. Dr. Matas had treated Bertha Thompson for tuberculosis of the spine at the Berwyn hospital. He told me "Ged, that was an impossible woman. She turned this hospital inside out and made life miserable for the staff whenever she came in. I tried to talk to her but it was useless. When she left it was as if a black cloud had lifted." Now I felt fairly certain that the Crown would call Barbara Bast and Dr. Matas as witnesses. That was why I wanted to talk to them before a subpoena was served. After my discussion I really thought that if the Crown prosecutor did not put them on the stand I might have to.

There was only one person who had a kind word for Mrs. Thompson and that was Mrs. Grover who lived on a nearby farm. She was a practical nurse. She would visit the Thompson place from time to time to help Bertha, give her baths, and tend to her needs.

After I had returned to my office, I learned the trial would be held early in the New Year and that Dr. Matas and Barbara Bast would be witnesses. I would make a case for Thompson from his voluntary statement to the police, and to a lesser extent from some of the Crown's witnesses, and my own address to the jury. We would be entitled to make the final argument because we were not calling any evidence.

In this instance such a result would be a potent plus for us. It is only when the defence does not call any evidence that counsel for the accused is put in such a favorable position. In the Thompson trial, the voice of counsel for the accused could be the voice *of* the accused, using *his* words in the statement, while explaining and emphasizing without danger of cross-examination or contradiction from Crown counsel. The judge would have a final say in his direction to the jury, but by then I knew Mr. Justice Tweedie would be presiding. From past experience I knew he would make sure the jury was aware it must not ignore portions of the Thompson statement that were favorable to the defence. There is always present in the minds of those who are involved as judges and counsel in criminal proceedings the centre piece of our system of criminal jurisprudence: *"a person is innocent until proven guilty—and guilt must be established beyond a reasonable doubt."* It is true this cardinal principle has been whittled away in some issues (mainly those where the fiscal policies of government are involved) but prosecutions under the criminal code must keep it in mind.

Nevertheless, as insurance I decided to bring in eight or nine of Thompson's neighbors. Moreover, by having these people and their families in for the several days of the trial, they would be mingling with others around the courthouse and in the hotels and cafes. At least part of their favorable feeling toward Harvey Thompson would rub off on the people they met.

So I drew up a list of these names and gave it to the RCMP to summon them.

Later, I was not only criticized by the deputy attorney general when I requested that the expenses of these potential defence witnesses be paid by the state, but met with an outraged refusal. Eventually, I complained to the local Member of the Alberta Legislature in the Social Credit government. He leaned on the bureaucracy and, in due course, witness expenses were met. A solicitor in the attorney general's office once told me they felt this was sharp practice on my part. I strongly disagree.

The Crown has access to all the resources it requires to obtain witnesses, including experts. They also have the police for detailed investigation and trained counsel to prosecute. Thompson was destitute and in debt. He was unable to pay me. I met certain disbursements from my own pocket. The Crown refused to accept him as an indigent case because the prosecution felt he had some equity in his soldier settlement land. He did, but not much. Years later it was sold and I received a small fee. I mention this because I believed that anyone charged with a serious crime was entitled to all the help that could be obtained.

Under normal circumstances, Harvey Thompson would have remained in custody until the spring assizes, but the authorities, faced with a docket of three murder trials as well as the usual assortment of civil and criminal actions, arrived at the sensible idea of holding a special sitting in January. The defendants in the three trials were Thompson; Jennie Robertson of the Whitelaw district (see pp. 114–123), arraigned for shooting her husband; and a Girouxville area farmer named Gougeon, held for murdering his wife.

I was acting for both Mrs. Robertson and Thompson. The Gougeon boys also asked me to undertake their father's defence. I decided it would be too difficult to handle them one after the other without a breathing space in between and suggested to the Gougeon family that defence be handled by another advocate, although I would assist and sit in for part of the trial.

The special sitting was gazetted with Mr. Justice Tweedie presiding, a jury list was drawn up, and its members summoned to appear for the mid-January, 1938, opening date. Although at that time reports of ominous stirrings in the old continent were reaching our land so far away from the feuds of Europe, the drama and emotion of the local murder cases to be tried took precedence over everything else. As a large number of spectators were expected, the Court was moved to the local movie theater where at 10:00 a.m. Monday morning, Mr. Justice Tweedie took his place on the improvised bench. Names appearing on the jury list were called. The three accused of murder, Mrs. Robertson, Mr. Gougeon, and Mr. Thompson were arraigned. All three pleaded not guilty and elected for trial by jury. I had asked the Crown prosecutor that, subject to the court's approval, Mrs. Robertson's case be tried first, then Gougeon's and, finally, Thompson's. This would give me time to brief Thompson and arrange the details of his defence. Most certainly I wanted him to understand the question of whether or not he should give evidence so he could share in the decision.

Mrs. Robertson's case was heard first and disposed of the following day.

Gougeon's defence was directed to the issue of his sanity. One evening he had loaded his .22 repeating rifle and calmly, in the presence of members of his family, repeatedly fired at his wife. There was no doubt the man was mentally disturbed. The lack of any immediate motive and his subsequent conduct established he was not sane by our usual standards. However, under the rigid definition of the criminal code, that was not enough to constitute insanity. I sat in on the Gougeon trial for a few hours and then went to see Thompson. That night I worked late in my office on his brief and thus was not aware of the result of the Gougeon trial.

I arrived in court early the next morning and was already gowned and seated at the counsel table when Thompson arrived with his RCMP escort. A constable tapped me on the shoulder, indicating my client wanted to see me. I went back to the prisoner's box to find Thompson slumped in his seat, looking pale and distraught.

"What's the matter, Harvey?" I asked.

"Did you hear about Gougeon?"

I shook my head.

"The police brought him down to the cells late last night after the trial. His cell's next to mine and he was crying and singing hymns. I saw him flop down on his knees and I called out, 'Gougeon, what is it?' He started crying and I heard him say 'thirty,' so I said, 'My God, did you get thirty years?' And he said, 'No, no. The jury found me guilty and I'll be hanged on March 30.' Mr. Baldwin, how will I do?"

I had only time to give him a reassuring pat on the knee before the judge was announced.

Jury selection was accomplished with remarkably little wrangling or dispute. It was a good cross-section of farmers and business people with no known hard-liners. The Crown called twelve witnesses. The first few were policemen to identify plans, photographers, the local doctor who had first been on the scene, and one or two other routine witnesses. Then the Crown called Mrs. Anna Grover, the Thompson's nearest neighbor.

Mrs. Grover spoke of visiting the Thompson house from time to time to assist Bertha. She said there were periods when Mrs. Thompson was bedridden and required some assistance, although most of the time she got around quite nicely with the aid of a walking stick. Under cross-examination, Mrs. Grover admitted that Bertha, while not a hypochondriac, tended to exaggerate and take advantage of her illness. She also said she was the one, after Thompson went to British Columbia, who had written him, urging he return and care for his wife. In hindsight, she said, it might have been better if she had not written.

Earl Grover, Mrs. Grover's son, was next in the witness box. He spoke of visiting the Thompson place with his mother the morning of December 4 and of finding the house burned. Under questioning he stated that Thompson and Bertha argued frequently and that Bertha was often abusive to her husband.

The following two witnesses were simply men who had driven with Harvey to Whitelaw where he had paid a debt from his grain check and then accompanied him to his farm. This was December 3. On neither trip did they enter the house or see Bertha.

Four witnesses were now left on the Crown list. What they had to say, how they said it, and how they responded to cross-examination was important.

The first was Corporal Harry Lowes, the investigating officer. He was closer to the case than any of the Crown people. I listened intently as he responded to questions by veteran Crown prosecutor, Sandy Phimester. Lowes's answers were crisp and detailed. He told of Thompson's arrest and the taking of his statement. He recalled that Thompson voluntarily told them of the events leading up to the killing and had repeated the statement two days later when it was taken down in writing. Both the written and oral statements, Lowes admitted, were for all practical purposes identical and so complete he had not questioned Thompson further. Lowes finished shortly before a scheduled adjournment, and I asked for and received permission to postpone my cross-examination until after the break.

During the brief adjournment I took aside two friends whose judgment I trusted for their assessment of the effect of Lowes's evidence. They thought as I did. Lowes had not said anything to cause the defence harm. They also agreed that Thompson's written statement had created a good bias toward him. One said to me, "No jury would convict a man of murder in the face of what we've just heard; it has to be manslaughter."

After adjournment the next two witnesses were Dr. Matt Matas and Corporal Walker of the Fairview detachment. Matas gave a very graphic and negative description of Mrs. Thompson's attitude during her stay in the hospital and I saw several jurors taking notes of his testimony. A straightforward, peppery man who always spoke his mind, irrespective of whom he was addressing, Matas was both liked and respected in the community. The Crown, anxious to nullify the effect of Thompson's statement that he had reacted in self-defence to a threat of harm from Mrs. Thompson, had called upon Matas as Bertha's physician to establish that the woman was too weak and ill to be feared by anyone. Under cross-examination, Dr. Matas stated that when Bertha Thompson was discharged, she was much stronger than upon admission.

Dr. John McGregor, the provincial pathologist, was the Crown's last witness. I had known Johnny McGregor since our public school days and held a high opinion of his integrity and professional skill. He had done a very detailed autopsy on the dead woman in Edmonton and diagnosed her illness as a tubercular hip. At the conclusion of his testimony, he mentioned in an almost casual way that Bertha had still been breathing when the fire was lit. Amazingly, Phimester let this go and I made only a perfunctory examination of McGregor.

In his statement, Thompson had described hearing his wife's death rattle. Both Dr. McFadyen and Dr. Matas had stated in a general way this could be possible. Matas had also said it was possible this movement had brought some smoke-filled air into the woman's system. I did not cross-examine McGregor on this dangerous subject. Later as John McGregor and I said goodbye before his departure for Edmonton, he laughed and told me, "I never got the chance to give the strongest part of my evidence as the department felt it would be more damaging if you initiated it."

During post-trial discussions I was given another interesting piece of information. The Crown had a surprise witness ready in the wings, but he was never called. The witness was a youth from the nearby town of Rycroft. He had been tried and convicted of stealing a quilt and sentenced to three months. While being conducted to Edmonton on the same train, he and Thompson had talked about some of the details of Bertha's death. It had been the Crown's intention to use the youth as a rebuttal witness when I called Harvey. Thus it appeared the department was in some doubt as to the kind of defence I would raise.

After McGregor left the stand, the Crown counsel rose to inform the court that the prosecution had finished its case. His Lordship turned to me. "Are you ready to proceed with your defence, Mr. Baldwin?" Events so far had followed the pattern I'd predicted. I saw no reason to call any witnesses. Thompson himself was terrified at the prospect of giving evidence. And why should he? Nothing he could say at this stage could improve on the story he had given the police. It was now part of the case for the prosecution. Certain Crown witnesses had helped him. In effect his best case had already been made by the prosecution. I replied, "My Lord, the accused will not be calling any evidence."

This put the ball squarely back in Phimester's court. He would be the first to make his final address to the jury. He squared his shoulders, told the court he was ready to proceed, and gave a first-class address. There were two main themes. First, Thompson had nothing to fear from his wife; thus, self-defence did not enter into the picture and the firing of the house was a clear sign of a guilty mind, bent on destroying the evidence of a vicious crime. Secondly, there was some evidence suggesting the woman was still alive when the fire started. Phimester concluded his address by calling for a verdict of murder. Unfortunately he labored his demand so strongly and at such length he lost his audience. I was to learn some months later that two jurors felt there should have been a complete acquittal.

I devoted a good portion of my address to going over Thompson's statement, sentence by sentence, trying to project the impression that Thompson himself was speaking the words. I also asked the jury to recall the assessment of Dr. McAlister, Thompson's examining psychiatrist. The husband, I told them, had for years treated with patience and good nature this woman who had caused him so much anguish. Then, finally, on the evening of December 3, the dam collapsed, letting loose all his resentment and bitterness. At the sight of Bertha Thompson crawling toward him, a knife in her hand, her face contorted with vicious anger, fear and rage caused him to lose control and react with violence.

My address lasted less than twenty minutes. Then it was the judge's turn. Tweedie gave the jury directions in simple but explicit terms. He outlined the possible verdicts, then came down as strongly as he could, within established precedents, for manslaughter. When he instructed the jury to retire, I was almost certain of the results of their deliberations. Favorably disposed toward the accused to begin with, the jury had now been told by the judge they were free to decide as they wanted.

The jury deliberated less than a half-hour before returning with a verdict of manslaughter and a special plea for leniency.

Mr. Justice Tweedie declared the sentence to be five years at the Prince Albert Penitentiary. The old theater was filled with subdued applause as spectators surged forward to wring Thompson's hand and wish him well.

Following the Thompson trial, we had two more days of civil and ordinary criminal dockets. Then it was all over. With relief we heard the clerk announce that all business being completed, court was adjourned.

The three murder trials had hung like a black cloud over the valley and it had been a difficult and strenuous time for all involved. No doubt it was this spirit of thankfulness that persuaded Judge Tweedie, a most convivial sort, to host a large party at his hotel, the old Victory. He extended a general invitation to everyone in any way connected with the proceedings—excepting, of course, the three who had been accused of murder. Tweedie made sure that ample refreshments and a first-rate lunch were laid on and it was one of the most interesting social events ever held in the dining room of the graceful old building. The evening did not end there. When the party broke up just after midnight, some of us were persuaded to continue on to the local curling rink. There were enough of us for six or seven rinks and I found myself on a rink with a farmer who had been a witness, an RCMP constable, and a juryman, curling against the rink skipped by the senior police official.

Only in the north!

The next day they had all gone—judge, court officials, press, police, witnesses, jury, and the three accused.

Jenny Robertson served only a year of her sentence before she was released. She did not return to the north. Gougeon had his death penalty commuted. While his mental condition had not brought him within the fine line of legal insanity, it was close enough to have the justice department officials who reviewed his file recommend that he not be hanged. His sentence was changed to life imprisonment and he died in an institution a few years later.

Thompson was a model prisoner and was free in a little over three years. I never saw him again as he went back to the United States. He wrote me and sent Christmas cards for several years. In his last letter he said he was living in a small city out west, had remarried, and was very happy.

The day after the trial I dragged myself out of bed and went to the office to see some clients and sort through the mail that had piled up over the past two weeks. As I drove to town, a thought came to mind that persisted on and off throughout the day. Here, in this small, isolated, northern community of Peace River, many people had gathered to see justice enacted. In particular, the system had decided the fate of three individuals—two men and one woman who faced the possibility of standing on the gallows waiting for the trap to spring and send their lives spinning into eternity. For this purpose, judges and lawyers in black gowns and white bibs, court officials mouthing the formal language of ancient days, technical experts, and others were called to testify. Many more were caught also in a web of time, all waiting for the moment when the jury would return with its verdict and the accused would be called to stand and hear his fate. These were the living. But what of the dead? Were they stage decorations, names fixed to a charge, only subjects of autopsies and inquests? What about poor Bertha Thompson?

Much of her life was no more than the usual mess of living—a hasty wartime marriage; a meagre honeymoon; then coming together again with a stranger; the harried struggle through a grinding depression; and, finally, the painful misery of a lingering illness. Today, it is not likely those two would ever have married; or, if they had, more liberal divorce laws would have allowed them to separate. Moreover, today our system of medicare and hospitalization would have treated and cured her illness. Unhappily, Bertha Thompson knew little but a wasted life.

I have ever been grateful that if we had to have a Great Depression, mine was spent in the north. I enjoyed my criminal work and sometimes I even got paid. Those of us who acted for the accused in the criminal courts were a sort of unpaid public utility. I never really minded because I believe anyone charged with a serious crime is entitled to all the help possible. The lasting friendships formed in those years were a real compensation for the lack of money; besides money-poor clients paid in other tender—moccasins, fur jackets, chickens. Once in a while a bootlegging client left a bottle of his best on our veranda!

Beulah and I financed the first house we ever built this way. An elderly man I defended on a charge of attempted murder insisted upon paying me with a good team of horses. This was something of a shocker. I had no means to care for horses, so I traded them for a set of building logs. Beulah and I then purchased three good river lots in West Peace River and began to build our first home. We obtained lumber, doors, and windows from W.E. Smith's sash and door mill as part payment of another legal debt. Some of our excavating, landscaping, and labor was paid for in the same way. Beulah and I helped with the shingling and the floor. The crowning glory of the house was a large fireplace. We built it from stones we found on the banks of the river and lugged home in our little boat. In the summer of 1933 we brought our first baby from the hospital to a brand-new home. True, the house did not have running water or electricity, but it was ours and completely paid for. I think we laid out less than $800 in cash.

CHAPTER FOUR

The Judge Said "Murder or Nothing"

THE SMALL HAMLET OF FAUST, LOCATED MIDWAY along the 75-mile south shoreline of Lesser Slave Lake, was one in a string of communities during the late 1920s and 1930s attractively situated and decorated with fine-sounding names—Slave Lake, Widewater, Canyon Creek, Driftpile, Kinuso, and Jussard. These places came into existence when the Northern Alberta Railway, which clung tightly to the lake's southern shore, was built. In compliance with the provisions of the Railway Act, sidings were established every seven miles or so. Out of these sidings grew many infant communities. Gradually the railway supplanted the wagon trails and lake vessels, providing a line of communications and nourishing the country it passed through. It was not until 1925 that construction was started on a graded dirt highway with culverts and bridges. It snaked beside the steel tracks and greatly increased the flow of traffic. Where early pioneers had toiled, sweated or frozen according to the season, manhandling their sleighs and wagons, people now talked of travelling from Edmonton to Grande Prairie or Peace River in *one day*—if it did not rain and if their vehicles held up. Nevertheless, despite the increase in vehicular traffic to the north country, there was no great change in the lives of people in the tiny villages dotting the shores of the lake. They continued to dwell in a quiet backwater of society.

Faust, with a small hotel, a few garages and service stations, three stores, and a poolroom, did have a modest economic link with the outside world with its fishing and fur farm industries during the 1920s and 1930s when Lesser Slave Lake was still

64

well-endowed with fish. Some of the fish was suitable for human consumption; a more coarse variety was used for feed by the local mink and fox farms. Until the lake was fished-out and the fish processing plants closed, Faust had been an attractive and moderately thriving community. Then came the Second World War.

There were enlistments and call-ups. Young men left the land. After the United States entered the war in 1941, the flow of traffic to the north thickened with vehicles carrying military personnel, civilians, and huge quantities of supplies to build, maintain, and defend the two big projects initiated by the Americans—the Alaska Highway and the Canol Pipe Line. With Canadian and American military units scattered throughout the north country, there was money, activity, and excitement!

The land changed, and the people with it, and not always for the better. For a few years after the war, the boom conditions lasted. A number of native families moved to Faust from the surrounding country or the area north of Lesser Slave Lake. Many of the men who were not called up found jobs on military projects in the Northwest Territories or the Yukon. Some joined the new fishing industry at Great Slave Lake. Generally the native women and children stayed on at Faust, and irregular liaisons were formed that cut across family lines. A jungle of tarpaper shacks and cabins sprang up, jammed together in the few hundred yards between the lake and the railroad tracks. It was mostly squatters' rights, with little regard for proper lot or road boundaries. The buildings were as temporary as the domestic arrangements of the men and women living in them.

In one of these shacks dwelt two adults and two children, all native. The adults were Mary Loyie, and her common-law husband, Martin Ouelette. Mary Loyie was still married to, but separated from, Victor Loyie of Lesser Slave Lake. One of the children, Leonard, was Mary's six-year-old son by her husband, Victor. The second child, a little girl of three, is assumed to have been fathered by Martin.

On the evening of March 27, 1947, a young woman named Lucy Cardinal paid a social visit to Martin and Mary's two-room shack. Lucy was living then with Nexton Erickson. She was twenty-six, about fifteen years younger than Mary, and she and

Mary had known each other almost six years. Martin had just returned to Faust from Hay River where he had been working in a
fish plant. He and Lucy had not known each other before.

The evening, which included a spot of drinking, passed without incident, although it appeared Lucy showed some interest in
Martin. When she left, she promised to come back the next day.
True to her word, the next afternoon about 3:00 p.m. she appeared at the door with a 26 oz. bottle of rum, which she coyly
announced she had brought "as a treat." Mary let her in, then
bustled around the small livingroom-kitchen, putting glasses,
hot water, and sugar on the table. When Martin, who had been
working outside the house, came in, the two women were sitting cozily at the table drinking hot rum. He joined them.

At first the talk was easy and friendly, touching on the people
in town and the fascinating subject of who was now living with
whom. Martin also spoke of his job and conditions in Hay
River. Up until that time that day there was no record of
domestic violence between Martin and Mary; but Martin's talk
of Hay River set Mary off on a string of complaints. She was sure
Martin must have been keeping another woman while he was
away. Mary had a foul tongue and a jealous temperament, and
could easily work herself into a passion after a few drinks.

Martin shot back that he was sure Mary had shacked up with
other men while he was up north, working hard to make enough
money to keep the family together.

From there the argument degenerated into a shouting,
screaming, and cursing match. Both Martin and Mary were
strongly built, muscular and stocky. They put on quite a show,
yelling and making threats while the children cowered in the
corner. Lucy stayed in the house, an interested spectator.

Eventually Lucy got up to leave, but Martin called to her,
"Come back here, I want to talk to you some more."

This was pure spite on his part. He was well aware that the
main cause of Mary's anger that evening was her jealousy of
Lucy Cardinal. Mary, in fact, left the cabin, saying, "Lucy, you
stay here with Martin. I'll go over and be Erickson's wife."

Simple, inexpensive divorce. Martin and Lucy were now in
the bedroom anyway.

Good as her word, Mary trotted to the Erickson cabin and
found Lucy's man alone, lying on the bed. Sitting down beside

him she told him what was on her mind. "Lucy is trying to get my man away from me. Maybe I had better stay here with you, and Martin can have her if he wants." Erickson, with a display of Scandinavian caution, said in effect, thanks, but no thanks. No doubt his reluctance was due in part to Mary's drunken condition. Mary stayed on in the cabin anyway. A short time later another neighbor, John Ward, arrived with his woman. Mary repeated her story to them, giving a blow-by-blow account of her domestic brawl with Martin. After a few drinks, Ward was persuaded to return with her to the shack to get Martin to listen to reason.

It is refreshing that at a time and place where wife beating was an accepted part of the domestic social condition, some sense of chivalry prevailed, even when mixed with rum.

Mary and Ward found Lucy with Martin in the small cabin, still drinking. Said John Ward, "What is wrong, Martin, beating your wife like that?"

Martin retorted, "I didn't start it. Mary is jealous on me about Lucy, and she wants to fight me about it."

Ward then took Martin Ouelette over to Erickson's place and a few minutes later Mary followed them. There was an attempt to patch up the quarrel, but it was not long before the shouting and insults erupted again. About 6:00 p.m., an RCMP car driven by Constable Macdonald, pulled up to the Erickson place. Macdonald, who was attached to the Slave Lake detachment, was on a patrol of Faust and Driftpile and had stopped to see Erickson and Lucy Cardinal. He knew nothing of anyone's domestic fight until he arrived at the cabin. Getting out of the car and walking toward the cabin, he heard shouting and cursing. Realizing there was little he could do, he started back to the car when Mary Loyie came flying out of the house, carrying a nearly empty bottle of rum, and yelling, "Martin Ouelette is a bootlegger. Money is being paid for liquor."

After a brief talk, interrupted when Ouelette tried to get in on the discussion, Mary then asked Constable Macdonald to drive her to Slave Lake. Thinking it was a good idea to separate the two, Macdonald agreed. He drove her to the downtown section of Faust, dropped her off, and promised to pick her up after he finished his patrol of Driftpile. Macdonald obviously figured he was witnessing no more than another drunken, family argument. He certainly had no belief at the time it would have a fatal ending. He was a good, conscientious policeman and would not have left if he had thought otherwise.

Martin Ouelette left the Erickson cabin some time after the policeman had driven away with Mary. He started back to his own home. A neighbor, Joe Cyre, saw Mary Loyie jump out at Martin and hit him with two sealers of fish. She knocked him down and when he got to his feet, knocked him down again. The two struggled on the ground for awhile, then Mary got to her feet and ran to the house of another neighbor, Gabe Gladue.

Over more drinks, Mary told the Gladues her troubles. Hoping Macdonald would have returned by now to Faust, she walked back into town with the Gladues. They went to the pool-room where John Bajer, the owner, spoke to them. Bajer was a witness at Martin's trial. He recollected that when they entered his place they made quite a fuss, laughing and talking loudly. He asked them to leave and they did so. When asked if they were quarrelsome and provocative, Bajer answered, "Not at all, they sang in a happy way." After looking around the little town for Macdonald, Mary and the Gladues headed back across the tracks.

Meanwhile, Martin had picked up the two children, who had somewhere along the line been left with another neighbor, and gone on home. Two hours later at 10:00 p.m., he banged at the door of Celeste Miskenack, his closest neighbor. Miskenack opened the door to find Ouelette standing outside with the two children. "My wife shot herself," he told Celeste. "I heard a shot, I woke up, and I looked over and saw Mary dead on the other bed." He gave the same terse statement to Macdonald later that same night.

Another member of the RCMP force, Constable Crawford of Slave Lake was on the passenger train passing through Faust at midnight. Word was sent to the station, and Crawford got off the train and walked to the Ouelette shack. He took charge of the investigation and interviewed Ouelette, after giving him the statutory warning. In the course of his conversation with Crawford, Martin made a lengthy, disjointed, rambling statement, detailing his problems with Mary. He added he had made up his mind to leave Faust by himself and go to the Queen Charlotte Islands where he could fish. He insisted that Mary had shot herself. Ouelette was taken into custody and transported to Peace River. A formal charge was laid against him for the murder of Mary Loyie.

March 31, after being in custody for three days, Martin Ouelette asked to see the subdivision commanding officer, Inspector Churchill. He made another statement. With only minor variations, it was plain he was staying with the story he had given earlier. The case nearly fitted a classical pattern. Two people are together; one is killed; there are no witnesses. To what extent is the story of the survivor accepted?

One of the prosecuting counsel was Don MacKenzie from the attorney general's Edmonton staff. After the trial MacKenzie wrote a memorandum explaining that the Crown pressed for a murder conviction rather than a manslaughter conviction because they knew that Ouelette had lied in some aspects of his story. That gave them reason enough they believed. However, the Crown is compelled to do much more than merely show a suspect has lied in some aspects to establish a positive case of murder. A long line of capital cases in the north where the prosecution had had a singular lack of success in securing murder convictions attested to faulty reasoning by the Crown. This one would be no different, although the Crown lawyers were able to persuade the judge of their point of view. I said the case nearly fitted a pattern. There was one difference. They did have a witness to the shooting—Leonard Loyie, six years old.

Late on the night of the shooting March 28, the police did question the boy, and again the next day. He said that Martin had shot his mother, that he had been inside the house, and that he "runned outside," but Martin had called him back.

There is a formidable obstacle to be overcome before the testimony of a young child can be received in court as evidence: It must be shown that the child understands the nature and solemnity of an oath and the consequences of lying after being sworn to tell the truth. Rarely is testimony taken from a child who has not been sworn.

Martin Ouelette's preliminary hearing was held in High Prairie about two weeks later. My father was retained for the defence while Sandy Phimester acted as agent for the attorney general.

Phimester attempted to have Leonard Loyie make a statement before the magistrate. The Crown admitted Leonard was too young to be sworn. He was put on the stand, however, in an attempt to show he was capable of making a statement. The attempt failed. The child did not respond even when asked his name, much less when asked if he knew what had happened to his mother.

Ouelette's initial statement to the police and all his subsequent statements were sufficient to commit Ouelette to trial at the Peace River Supreme Court. The child's evidence was not needed, although another attempt was made to secure a statement from Leonard at the trial itself. This time the judge took an active part in the questioning, but the little fellow remained unable to tell what he had seen and heard the night his mother was shot.

It is now possible to peer through the thick underbrush of varying statements, contradictory reports, assumptions and educated guesses covering the ground at the time of the preliminary hearing and speculate about what really happened in the little shack on the shores of Lesser Slave Lake that night.

Obviously Mary Loyie did not meet her death by suicide. But was it downright murder, complete with intent and premeditation? Or, was it an accident—a gun discharging in the course of a struggle?

The view put forward by the Crown was that Martin Ouelette formed an intention to kill Mary Loyie, went home, loaded the gun, and deliberately shot her down when she entered the house. To sustain this theory the police offered in evidence the request Ouelette had made to the wife of a neighbor about looking after the children. According to the police, Martin was arranging for the care of his children because he intended to murder his wife and then leave the province.

There was another minor aspect. Examining the cabin after the shooting, Constable Macdonald found Mary Loyie lying on one bed and the gun nearby. There were a number of shells scattered in a disorderly pile on the bed. Most were 12 gauge, but a few were 20 gauge. The gun that killed Mary took 20 gauge. Surely Ouelette knew that. Perhaps Mary did not if it was she who had loaded the shotgun, pawing through the box to find a shell that would fit.

Moreover, Mary had arranged for a ride to Slave Lake with Macdonald. She had even put some of her things in the patrol car. Martin knew this. He himself had made up his mind to leave Faust, too.

My surmise is Mary Loyie returned to the house still filled with her grievances, and the fight started again. Martin reacted, the loaded gun came into the picture, there was a fierce battle for its possession, and it discharged. The police expert suggested the shot was fired from two to four feet from the body.

Although a jury can find for either murder or manslaughter, the attorney general must decide what charge is to be laid. The authorities decided to press for murder. Their case was dependent on Ouelette's somewhat conflicting statements, the story told by little Leonard, and Lucy Cardinal's colored evidence.

On June 25, 1947, 10:00 a.m., Martin Ouelette came face to face with a judge and jury. The judge was Mr. Justice Campbell McLaurin from Calgary. My father, V. R. Baldwin, and his partner, Claude Campbell, appeared for the accused. It was a good jury, not made up of people with a bias for the prosecution or the defence, nor were they the type of men to take kindly to any judge's attempt to strong-arm them into a verdict they did not like.

The case for the prosecution generally followed the pattern of the first hearing in High Prairie.

Lucy Cardinal was a principal witness for the Crown. Her evidence was not entirely unbiased. Like many who become witnesses under such circumstances, she was anxious to show herself in the best possible light. There were obvious discrepancies in the stories she told to the police and her sworn testimony at the preliminary hearing and the supreme court trial. For example, she volunteered that she had brought a bottle of rum to the shack on the afternoon of March 28th, but denied anyone was drunk. When there was talk of bootlegging, Lucy shifted her story to say that Martin and Mary were already drinking rum when she arrived at the shack.

Lucy also stated that both Martin and Mary struck each other, and Martin knocked the woman down twice. Once he picked up a kitchen knife and waved it at Mary. He also pointed a hammer at her and threw a kitchen tumbler, not at her but against the wall. Another time he took a small penknife from his pocket and held it at Mary's throat, although he did not touch her with it.

Lucy, however, stated that, acting as peacemaker, she had no trouble in disarming Martin and taking the various weapons from him. She explained that she pulled at his sleeve until it tore, then took the kitchen knife and put it behind the radio. She also made him close the small penknife and return it to his pocket. Not one of the weapons was used to make contact with Mary. Lucy was much smaller and lighter than Martin. If it had been his intention to harm Mary, she could not have prevented it.

It was undoubtedly a fierce quarrel; but I believe the Crown made a grave mistake in attempting to show that these actions of Martin's formed the basis of an intent to kill Mary Loyie. Common sense surely dictated that a muscular and heavy-set individual like Martin Ouelette, inflamed by rage and liquor, could not have been so easily disarmed by Lucy, a much smaller person, had he been really set on doing serious injury to Mary, his woman.

There was very little evidence offered by the defence. A few friends and neighbors told of the problems between Martin Ouelette and Mary Loyie and of her aggressive nature under the influence of drink. Certain of Ouelette's statements were read, but he did not take the stand.

Lucy Cardinal's evidence and the written statement by Ouelette fell far short of the standard of proof required to show premeditation or intent on the part of Ouelette to kill the woman. If anything they pointed in the opposite direction suggesting the shooting was more the result of an impulse of the moment rather than a planned assassination.

Lucy Cardinal did not improve on her performance at the preliminary hearing and when her cross-examination was completed, it was difficult for the Crown to contend that the fight at the Ouelette cabin was certain to be followed by murder.

Yet the lawyers for the Crown, following the instructions in their brief, kept boring in on the subject of deliberate murder.

In his summation to the jury, Mr. MacKenzie made a powerful pitch for a murder conviction. The judge followed with a direction using even stronger language. Nevertheless, my father pointed out to the jury that only it may be the sole arbiter of the facts. The jury kept that in mind. The judge said, "Murder or nothing." The jury said, "Nothing." Martin Ouelette left the courtroom in Peace River a free man.

Years later a member of that jury told me a big factor in persuading them to deliberately reject the Crown's position was the sternness of the judge's admonition that murder was the only verdict possible.

One other piece of evidence was in favor of the accused. The RCMP ballistics expert, Sergeant Mason-Rooke, admitted under cross-examination that the makeshift trigger device of the shotgun made it possible for the weapon to be discharged without anyone actually pulling the trigger. It was held together by a rubber band. This lent substance to Ouelette's claim that the gun went off during his struggle with Mary. Peace River jurymen would have appreciated the significance of that information about the trigger, no matter what the judge thought about it all.

CHAPTER FIVE

The Case of the Vanishing Corpse

IN JANUARY 1935, WILLIAM BYRD, A SMALL FARMER FROM the Fairview district, made a visit to Edmonton where he met a young German immigrant named Martin Poepper. The two men had little in common. Byrd, a thin, spare man of middle years with a lined face and close-set eyes, was somewhat of a loner, living by himself in a shack on his farm. He had two or three cronies from among Fairview's less reputable element, but even these he saw only from time to time. Moreover, he was known for his sudden and violent temper and it was rumored he had come north because of brushes with the law in the United States. By contrast, Poepper was big, red-faced, and bombastic. He was a great talker, full of tall tales in his broken English about his earlier life in Germany. Despite their differences, the two men held one interest in common, Byrd's farm. From what I could gather, Byrd was not much of a farmer, and had little interest in his land. I believe he was simply marking time, scratching a meagre living from the farm while waiting out the Depression.

Poepper on the other hand was ambitious and wanted farmland. He expressed great interest in the agricultural conditions of the Fairview area, and painted a glowing picture of his farming experience and capabilities. He may also have led Byrd to believe he had access to enough money to get started on the land. This was utter nonsense. Poepper had neither resources nor hope of finding any in the near future.

Within a short time of their meeting, the men reached an understanding. Byrd wanted someone to help with the farm and it was agreed that Poepper would work for him, at least until the spring crop was in. At the same time he would look the situation over. They left Edmonton together by train, arriving in Fairview the first day of February, 1935, and drove to Byrd's farm. It was located some ten miles northwest of Fairview by the Hines Creek coulée, a wide, deep gash in the surrounding plateau. The two settled in at the small shack, sharing the chores and preparing for spring seeding.

At first they managed to get along nicely; so much so that six days after their arrival, they went to Fairview and made a contract by way of a printed lien agreement. This was a form needing only the insertion of the names and description of the property to be completed. It dealt with the sale of Byrd's household goods, farm equipment, and stock to Poepper. It was an unusual agreement, especially as they had known each other for such a short time. No provision was made for the use of the house. They must have intended that, for the time being, both would stay on—Byrd owning the land and shack but Peopper having an interest in the contents.

The purchase price was fixed at $1,000. Even during the Depression, that was a very moderate sum for the entire contents of the house, the stock, and all the farm machinery, including the truck. No cash was exchanged at the signing of the document. The money was to be paid in five yearly instalments, starting at the end of the current year. The debt of $1,000 carried no interest.

Although Byrd would never admit to me he had been taken in by Poepper's stories about his farming experience and his ability to raise money, I am convinced this was the case. I am equally convinced Byrd felt he would be able to sell his land to Poepper at a very good price in the near future. I tried to get to the bottom of the deal after Byrd retained me to act for him, but he hedged and equivocated, largely because he disliked admitting he had been made to look a fool. According to Poepper, the deal was that Byrd would let him farm the land on a crop share basis.

It did not take long for Byrd to realize he had made a bargain-basement sale of his property, even for the year 1935. Moreover, in doing so he had crippled himself in his capacity to work his own farm. He owned the land and cabin; but all the equipment and stock needed to operate the place, even the furnishings in his home, now belonged to Poepper. Under such circumstances, only two people of compatible and congenial natures could live together in harmony. These two certainly did not meet that test.

The surly, withdrawn Byrd now found himself confined in a little shack with a man he thought a loud-mouthed braggart and, moreover, one who had placed him in an impossible business situation. It was only natural there would be irritations, quarrels, and bickering and these would increase with each passing day.

In their statements and in the evidence given later in court, Byrd and Poepper told different stories about the frequency and nature of their quarrels. Byrd magnified the difficulties and insisted Poepper instigated the quarrels and made constant threats against him. Poepper downgraded the incidents.

The quarreling was an important secondary issue at Byrd's trial and my judgment was to go along with him, not because he was my client, but because his story was more consistent with what later transpired. Poepper struck me as the sort of man who would browbeat his opponent in order to get his own way.

By the end of March they could not delay longer in seeding the land, and a full-scale dispute erupted about who was going to pay for this. There was a material change in the situation when Poepper wrote and persuaded a young friend, Herman Wulff, to join him in Fairview. Wulff, in his early twenties, was from the Dapp area about 70 miles north of Edmonton where Poepper had spent some time. Apparently, Poepper was romantically involved with Wulff's sister. I imagine Poepper wrote convincingly about how good conditions were in the north and the prospects of getting a homestead. Poepper probably felt he needed someone in his corner and, even more, help with the farming in case Byrd left.

In any event, young Wulff arrived in the latter part of April and moved into the cabin with Poepper and Byrd. His presence served to drive a further wedge between the two. As so often happens with the introduction of a third party, people in opposition tend to take harder, inflexible positions, and small, simple issues assume larger and more complex proportions. Certainly, after Wulff arrived, hardly a day went by without some violent argument breaking out.

At twenty-three, Herman Wulff conducted himself like a much younger lad. Most of his life had been spent on the family farm at Dapp and he had not seen much of the world. About five foot, eight inches in height and slightly built, he had an obvious attachment to Poepper, based on their former friendship and the older man's relationship with his sister.

Not long after Wulff appeared on the scene, William Byrd took a specific initiative to deal with the problem. He went to Fairview one day and paid a visit to Constable Sanbrooke, then in charge of the Fairview RCMP detachment. Byrd was known to Sanbrooke and it's safe to say the man did not have a particularly high profile with the force. He complained to Sanbrooke about Poepper, saying: "He's always looking for fights. He's threatened me, and I'm really afraid of him. I think he's crazy and I want you to take him away out of my house. Get him to the Ponoka asylum where they can look after him." Sanbrooke questioned Byrd, but said in his report that he did not place too much reliance on the story. He did, however, take Byrd to see the local justice of the peace Ed Martin, who was also the secretary-treasurer of the rural Municipal District of Fairview, a good solid citizen, later to be the M.L.A. for the constituency of Fairview. Martin had a wide fund of information about people and conditions in the district. Martin listened patiently while Byrd ran through his list of complaints. He pointed out there was not really enough corroborated evidence to make a case for having Poepper bound over to keep the peace. Further, he doubted very much if there could be a committal under provincial insanity laws. For that matter, under existing regulations, he would require certificates from two qualified medical practitioners. A cautious official, Martin quite properly pointed out that he was giving only an opinion and not a judgment. If Byrd wanted to swear out an information, Martin would take it and set in motion the required proceedings.

Byrd hesitated. He wanted badly to be free of Poepper, but in the end he decided against starting anything because of the possible consequences if the action were abortive.

I was never able to decide if Byrd really was alarmed or if he was just seeking a simple way to free himself from a miserable entanglement. Perhaps he was trying to build a case against Poepper if there should be trouble in the future.

Several days later on Saturday, May 10, the three men decided to take advantage of a fine, sunny day to cross over the coulée and look for some land that had just come open as a possible homestead for Wulff. At Poepper's suggestion they took guns so they could hunt along the way. Byrd owned a rifle and a shotgun, and they had borrowed another rifle from a neighbor some days earlier.

They set out from the shack about noon, angling down the Hines Creek coulée bank, intending to find a suitable spot to ford the creek, then climb the hill on the other side. However, heavy rains had so swollen the usual spring run-off, they could not find a safe place to cross. The coulée runs in a general north-south direction, cutting into the Peace River close to Dunvegan about 15 miles southwest of Fairview, getting deeper as it approaches the river. In some places the creek is several hundred feet below the level of the surrounding plateau and the hills on both sides are roughly contoured with a heavy covering of brush and clumps of trees. The creek varies from a mere trickle in late summer to a swift flood in spring when the winter run-off and early rains create a heavy rush to the Peace.

The men made their way slowly and with difficulty along the side of the creek. Each time Poepper suggested a crossing place, Byrd insisted it was not safe. Poepper began taunting the other man, jeering because he was so easily scared, accusing him of being miserable and ornery. So far they had spotted no game. Finally, after several hours of slipping and sliding along the coulée bottom, Wulff spotted and shot a game bird. After another hour of slow going, the party came upon a large spruce thicket. Poepper, who was in the lead, called back that this looked a good place to see deer. He started toward the trees. Byrd was scornful, commenting, "I know this place pretty well. There's never been a deer or any other big game through here."

Poepper answered angrily that Byrd was always opposing him and he was going to hunt through the bush. At this stage Martin Poepper was some twenty paces in the lead carrying a Winchester. Next came Byrd with his .32 rifle, while Wulff, who had the shotgun, walked about ten yards behind him.

Different versions were given as to some of the facts during the course of this expedition. But there was no dispute as to what happened next.

As Poepper, turning to talk to Byrd, changed his position and commenced walking toward the thicket, Byrd raised his rifle and shot him in the back of the head. Poepper fell heavily to the ground and lay motionless. Young Wulff stood rooted to the spot in fear and horror. Finally Byrd harshly ordered him to pick up the rifle which had fallen from Poepper's shoulder and Wulff did as he was bid. The two men turned and started slogging toward the farm. Neither examined Poepper to see if he was still alive.

The shooting took place about 6:00 p.m. Even though they were tired the two made better time on the return trip. Byrd kept urging Wulff to move faster and they stayed on the few trails and paths known to the older man. Reaching home about two hours later, they paused only to snatch a quick meal and feed and water the stock. Then they made their way back to the spruce thicket. This time they took a grub hoe and a couple of shovels with them; Byrd carried his rifle.

There isn't the slightest doubt that Byrd, believing he had killed Poepper, intended to bury the corpse.

Where did young Wulff fit into all this?

The police developed the theory, as policemen will, that after Poepper's body had been disposed of, Byrd planned to shoot and bury Wulff, the only witness. Byrd stoutly denied this.

Later, when I questioned him closely, he insisted he had no intention of harming the boy, and he may have been telling the truth. Now if Wulff had indicated he intended to report the shooting, or had tried to oppose Byrd it might have been a different story. But the young fellow apparently made no move to do this. He did what Byrd told him to do without protest. He was young, and he was terrified. Byrd had shown the hard, ruthless side of his character, and the weaker boy had simply gone along with him.

In darkness, carrying the gun and tools, the two men struggled back wearily over the rough terrain until they reached the scene of the shooting.

And there they discovered that the body of Martin Poepper was missing!

Frantically they searched the area, combing the bush and creek sides, but no Poepper. It became clear Poepper had not been killed. He must have revived and either fallen into the creek or wandered somewhere along the coulée. They continued the search, but Poepper was not to be found.

There was nothing to do but pick up the grub hoe and other tools and return to the farm. As they once again headed toward the shack, it became increasingly clear to Byrd that he must make some report of the incident to the authorities. So, as soon as he and Wulff reached the farm, they saddled two horses and rode into Fairview, arriving at about 5:00 a.m., but stopping first at the shack of James Bagley, one of Byrd's old cronies.

Bagley lived on the fringes of town in more ways than one. He had appeared as a witness in several of my cases and was reputed to have some knowledge as to the operation of the law. He often advised his friends about the labyrinth of the courts, police, and Liquor Control Act.

Shortly after 7:00 a.m., on the morning of Sunday, May 11, Byrd showed up at the RCMP station and told Constable Sanbrooke of the shooting of Martin Poepper. He said he had only done so in self-defence after being threatened. Sanbrooke questioned him closely, then took a statement. Byrd was not placed under arrest at the time, as Sanbrooke contended he did not yet have enough information to allow him to form an intention of taking him into custody, a very narrow judgment. Thus, the statement was not preceded by the customary statutory warning.

Now let us return to Martin Poepper, left for dead at the coulée bottom. He had regained consciousness about an hour after the others left and was able to raise himself to his knees. Then clinging to a bush, he struggled to his feet. He said later he had no memory of the shot being fired.

He found he was bleeding from the nose, mouth, and back of the head, and tried to stop the flow with his handkerchief. He then thought he had more strength and could move slowly on foot. Stumbling and staggering he made his way along the coulée bottom, up the steep bank, and on to the farm of Byrd's neighbour, W.E. Parliament—all this in the dark of night in thickly wooded, rough, and unfamiliar territory.

Fortunately for Poepper, Parliament was outside his house when he saw a figure moving erratically along a plowed field, then trip and fall between two furrows. Parliament ran to where the now unconscious man lay bleeding from the back of his head. He turned him over. In a few minutes Poepper revived and was able to talk. He told Parliament he was living at William Byrd's place. They had been hunting and he had found himself lying on the ground with blood on his face and on the ground around his head. Parliament asked Poepper why he had not gone to Byrd's place, which was closer, Martin answered, "I was afraid if I went back they would finish me off." He then asked if he'd been shot, adding, "If I was, Bill Byrd did it."

Parliament half carried, half dragged Poepper into the house, gave him what first-aid he could, then sent to Fairview for Dr. Wright.

One of the doctors who examined Poepper told me shock and loss of blood would probably have finished Poepper if he had stopped to lie down. I cannot leave this part of the account without reflecting that Poepper's remarkable survival is an example of the will to live. Part of his aggressive and dogged nature had brought him to his feet and kept him moving across the difficult terrain and along the creek and then had made him drag himself up the steep slope and through the ploughed fields to the Parliament farm.

Young Herman Wulff was a key figure in the trial of William Byrd for the attempted murder of Martin Poepper and what he said and did is of some importance. Keeping in mind his limited experience and naive ways, it is only natural he would be paralyzed by fear and shock after watching Byrd lift his rifle and shoot Poepper in the head. Even so it is still not easy to explain his failure to make any attempt to find out the extent of Poepper's injuries. Wulff made two widely differing statements to the police. First, he confirmed Byrd's account of the shooting. Then, in his next interview, Wulff contended that Byrd told him to say Poepper had left the country and gone away somewhere, and had backed this direction with a stern warning about what would happen if he disobeyed.

This was not a closely settled area. Poepper had not been around very long, had made no friends, and as Byrd figured, probably correctly, he would not be missed. It was unlikely anyone would inquire after him.

According to Wulff's first statement to the police, Poepper made threatening gestures with his rifle as he started to move into the bush, and immediately following this action Byrd had lifted his rifle and shot the other man. This was what Byrd had told the police and what Wulff repeated, but later he retracted it and told a different story.

In spite of a great many years in my profession, I have never found it easy to burrow into another person's mind and understand the mental processes which caused, preceded, or accompanied an act of violence.

Byrd was a hard case and had had serious problems with Poepper. Yet I do not think he had come to a firm decision to eliminate Poepper, or had even contemplated doing so because it was Poepper who had proposed the expedition, and it was Poepper who had suggested they take guns along. At the same time it was impossible not to know that Byrd and Poepper thoroughly detested each other. Then it is necessary to weigh the differences between the two men. Poepper was loud and abrasive and might utter threats as a form of bullying. Byrd, on the other hand, would not say much but was a much more dangerous man. One might threaten, the other would act. It was possible Byrd had given Poepper's threats more substance than they deserved.

There is another aspect. After Wulff and Byrd came to town to report the incident, Wulff stayed with Bagley while Byrd went alone to the RCMP barracks to tell his story. According to Bagley, young Herman said after Byrd left, "The story I told you with Byrd is right. Martin did threaten Bill twice that day by swinging his rifle at him." He gave the same version when he was questioned by the police.

Sanbrooke did not believe him and the next day went after the lad strongly, challenging, and cross-examining him. It was only after Wulff had learned Poepper was in the Fairview hospital and would recover that he reversed his story, and claimed he had lied because he was in fear of Byrd.

Wulff was, in fact, the key to the whole case!

I had a chance to question Wulff at the preliminary hearing held in Fairview, May 31. He was a very bad witness. He stammered, hesitated, made mistakes; but, on the whole, I was satisfied that he had been desperately afraid of Byrd that night. Could he really have seen in detail the gestures of both men just before Poepper was shot?

After the hearing I went to the coulée and climbed down to examine the site of the shooting. The police had been there and removed the handkerchief Poepper had used to check the flow of blood and other evidence. The area was well marked. Checking the data supplied to me, I had to accept Wulff's story that he could see both men. On the other hand, it was rough country. Anyone afoot would have had to look frequently at the ground to keep from stumbling. Either Poepper or Byrd could have made quick threatening motions without being observed by young Wulff. Putting two and two together it is not impossible to believe that Byrd might have thought Poepper had threatened him and had thereupon shot him. Further, believing Poepper to be dead, Byrd might have set about getting rid of the evidence.

Curiously enough, it would have been difficult to secure a murder conviction if Poepper had in fact died. The Crown prosecutor would have been driven to rely on Wulff as the principal prop of his case and without Poepper to confirm the testimony, the Crown's whole case was likely to have come unstuck. Even a conviction for manslaughter would have been difficult to secure.

In his initial interview with Sanbrooke, Wulff had stated, "Martin got mad and started cursing him. Martin pumped a shell into his gun and pointed it at him." During the same interview, which was taken down in writing, Wulff told of other threats Poepper had made on different occasions and how he had passed information about these on to Byrd.

When Wulff changed his story the next day, it was during an interview by Sanbrooke and another officer, Inspector Radcliffe from Peace River. Wulff now claimed that soon after the three men started toward the thicket, Byrd pointed his rifle at Martin and shot him. Poepper, he claimed, had never threatened Byrd. Wulff also said he was frightened of Byrd and did not want to take any chances, although he did not think the older man would actually have shot him.

It is my feeling that when Wulff swung over to Poepper's side, he was filled with remorse over his treatment of his friend. He had left him lying on the ground, he had even defended the man who had shot him. Now a strong reaction had set in, causing him to place Byrd in the worst possible light. Wulff struck me as a person controlled by events outside his capacity.

After Wulff's statement was taken an information was sworn against Byrd for attempted murder and he was arrested and taken to Peace River.

Poepper's injuries were serious and it was a few days before his doctor felt it was safe to remove the bullet, but he was expected to survive. Several weeks, however, would pass before he was able to appear for a preliminary hearing and Byrd was kept in the north awaiting the event.

Byrd sent for me after his arrival in Peace River and asked me to represent him. He said he was without funds to pay me and had no hope of obtaining any. His personal belongings were under contract to Poepper and nobody would be seriously interested in his farm which was under mortgage. I took the case, hoping to persuade the attorney general's department to make some contribution toward my fee.

I wrote promptly to Mr. George Henwood, the head of the department, and the man to whom I had been articled just before being admitted to the bar. At the time there was a general retrenchment underway in the department and I was met with a curt refusal, coupled with an explanation that, with the exception of capital crimes, it was only in the most exceptional cases that counsel would be retained for a criminal defence. I wrote back saying I would consider my position and let them know whether or not I would take the case. I knew there was more than one way to skin a cat. It was not the money and I knew I would be appearing in any event. It was the high-and-mighty attitude of the bureaucracy which got under my skin, just as it did many years later when I got into elective politics.

During my several interviews with Byrd he confessed he had made several statements to the police and was afraid there were substantial variations in what he had said. By now we knew Wulff had joined the prosecution team and would be testifying against Byrd. Although Byrd had not planned the hunting expedition as a means of ridding himself of the troublesome German, it was difficult after reviewing the evidence to escape the compelling conclusion that he had been quick off the mark to take advantage when given the opportunity.

Equally it would be hard to persuade a jury that he had believed his life to be in danger. Nor would the bad blood between the two or Poepper's threats just prior to the shooting be a legal defence, and there was no emotional peg on which to appeal to the feelings of an average northern jury. In fact it would be downright difficult to establish out of the mouth of a witness like Byrd his particular relationship with Poepper and how it was linked to the shooting. That might influence the sentence, but it would be no basis for a not guilty verdict. I explained all this to Byrd as best I could and rammed home to him that we faced a serious problem because he had planted several different stories with the police. Under these conditions, I thought we would do better without a jury. He agreed.

By now I was receiving almost daily telephone calls from the agent for the attorney general, who would be conducting the prosecution, asking if I was committed to the case and, more important, would a jury be required? These inquiries showed which way the wind was blowing. The department wanted the trial disposed of at the forthcoming June assizes. Certainly they were not anxious to be put in the position of keeping a man in jail for many months without trial when there was an opportunity to dispose of his case. Phimester, the Peace River Crown prosecutor, realized this and knew very well that if a jury was required for the June sittings, it would have to be called at once. To draw up a large enough panel and serve each member with a summons took some time. It was also costly and would put the authorities in Edmonton to the expense of several thousand dollars and much trouble.

When I told him I could not say if I was even appearing at Peace River's supreme court in June, he understood the situation and telephoned the officials in Edmonton. The next day he received a grudging approval for me to be retained by the province as counsel for William Byrd. Most graciously I thanked the department and advised Phimester that my client had instructed me to dispense with a jury.

Today when millions of dollars are disbursed each year in legal aid, it seems unbelievable that a justice department could act in such a penurious manner; however, this was 1935, a different age. I ultimately received a fee of something less than $100, which barely covered my expenses.

I saw Poepper for the first time at the preliminary hearing before Magistrate Stewart. Poepper was a very nervous young man, who kept darting glances to where Byrd sat guarded by an

RCMP constable. At one time, one of the rifles put into evidence fell from the table to the floor with a loud clatter. Poepper jumped from his chair, crouched on the floor covering his head with his arms, and screamed, "Has Bill got a rifle? Keep him away!" It was pretty strong stuff and quite convincing. Martin Poepper wanted as little to do with William Byrd as possible.

The only witness I leaned on was young Herman Wulff. I needed to check his capacity to rationalize the two different stories he had given the police. In particular there were four points to check: After his friend was shot, why did he not check to find out if Poepper was dead? Had the police pressured him to alter his story to conform to their theory? When he was left alone with Bagley after Byrd had gone to the police, why had he not told Bagley the truth, then gone to the police on his own? Finally, was he able to keep Poepper in constant observation when the latter started forward into the spruce thicket?

On the stand, Wulff was a terrible witness. He stammered, hesitated, equivocated; but he stubbornly stuck to the basic version of his story and swore he was terrified of Byrd. He only told the truth when reassured of his safety. I could only guess after it was all over that his evidence under oath was basically what had happened, although the police might have induced him to polish his story up somewhat. The more I hammered Wulff on the stand, the more he persisted in his story. It is possible his naiveté and simpleness buttressed my perception of his truthfulness.

After the preliminary inquiry and following intensive investigations and conversation with many people in the district, I was reasonably certain William Byrd would be found guilty. The main issue now was what would be the length of the term of imprisonment?

The luck of the judicial lottery brought Mr. Justice Ives to Peace River in June to preside over the supreme court cases set down for hearing at that time. Ives was a slight, somewhat stooped man, laconic in manner, with a tendency to lounge on the bench, so that quite often all we could see from where we sat at the counsel table was his big-domed bald head, with his glasses pushed back. The press sometimes called him the "Cowboy Judge" because he had at one time punched cattle in southern Alberta. Ives was one of the few judges I knew who

"Ged" Baldwin

Beulah

Parade, May 24, 1922. Main Street, Peace River, showing the Empire Theatre, scene of the Bradley trial. (Provincial Archives of Alberta: Photograph Collection A9868.)

Main Street, Peace River, 1929. My office is in the centre of the block.

Major A. E. C MacDonnell. (Peace
River Centennial Museum and Archives 77.767.19.)

Mr. Justice (later Lieutenant-Gov-
ernor) Walsh. (Provincial Archives
of Alberta: Pollard Collection
P5221.)

Judge T. M. Tweedie (left) being sworn in as Chief Justice, Trial Division, by Chief Justice Harvey, 1944. (Provincial Archives of Alberta:
Alfred Blyth Collection BL780/1.)

The supreme court sitting, Peace River, in Boyd Theatre, Mr. Justice Shepherd presiding. Counsel (left to right) *V. R. Baldwin, M. W. MacDonald, G. W. Baldwin, J. A. Olivier;* (behind, seated) *Court Reporter Barnett;* (standing) *the litigant and RCMP Constable Allen.*

Judge Noel with members of judicial party prior to departure from Peace River on judicial trip to Fort Vermilion. Inspector (then Sergeant) Anderson at the back right. (Peace River Centennial Museum and Archives 73.568.63.)

Fort Vermilion, showing boat tied up at bank. (Provincial Archives of Alberta: Photograph Collection A5383.)

Vessel D. A. Thomas *taking on wood for fuel. (Provincial Archives of Alberta: Photograph Collection A5050.)*

Peace River vehicle bridge, from west looking east toward the town.
(Peace River Centennial Museum and Archives 79.1058.1.)

Peace River bridge showing a car that skidded and struck the fence.
(Peace River Centennial Museum and Archives 80.1129.9.)

Part of Peace River town in 1915. The jack pine flat can be seen on the opposite bank. (Provincial Archives of Alberta: Photograph Collection A9867.)

The battle for the recognition of rapeseed (1960–61). Group of Western MPs on steps of the Centre Block, Parliament Buildings, that went with me as witnesses to the Board of Transport Commissioners' hearings.

Laying of rails into the Northwest Territories August 29, 1964. Mr. Roger Graham, Vice-President of Canadian National Railways, is at the microphone, accompanied by the Hon. Arthur Laing, Minister for Northern Affairs. I am on Mr. Graham's immediate right. (Canadian National Railways.)

did not interfere with the handling of a trial by counsel. He rarely took any action to examine a witness on his own. He was most observant and little escaped him. Ives had a first-rate capacity to assess human nature, and his evaluation of the facts was rarely wrong.

The trial was brief, lasting just one day. It was more or less a rerun of the earlier preliminary hearing, except that I had a little more success in my questioning of Wulff. I was able to confront him with the evidence given at the Fairview trial which, in some instances, was not consistent with what he testified to at Peace River. In addition, more emphasis was placed on Bagley's evidence about what Wulff had told him about Poepper's threats.

When the evidence was all in, I had the idea the judge was not greatly impressed by either side. However, there was a clear case that the accused had shot Poepper with no lawful provocation. After the last witness had left the box, Mr. Justice Ives made no attempt to sum up the evidence, but in his customary terse way, he wasted no time finishing the matter, saying in effect: "I find you guilty and sentence you to three years in the penitentiary. In doing so, I am taking into account that Poepper was not an easy man to get along with. But neither that nor your dispute over your agreement gave you the license to shoot. Let me also say that if this man had died, it is quite likely a jury would have found you guilty, and I would now be sentencing you to death, and that sentence would have been carried out."

After Byrd was taken away, I saw him only once more in connection with a civil action Poepper brought against him for damages. Byrd was brought from jail for the trial. Judgment went against him, although I doubt if Poepper obtained anything but the farm equipment, stock, and the equity Byrd had in the land. Poepper stayed around for awhile after disposing of the property, then, as far as I know, he too left the country. I know I rarely cross the Hines Creek coulée without thinking of the desperate, stumbling trip Poepper made that cold, dark, spring night after being left for dead.

CHAPTER SIX

The Case of the Naked Runner

NEW YEAR'S EVE, 1946 IN PEACE RIVER WAS HARSH, biting cold, with temperatures falling to -40° F. In the small farming community of Girouxville, 50 miles south of Peace River, much of the jollity, partying, and visiting back and forth between neighbors that normally would have marked the holiday in this close French-Canadian district was cut out. Most farmers thought it best to stay home and keep the fires going. The family of Victor Leclerc, a farmer in the area, had stayed up until midnight, more to keep the stoves well supplied with fuel than to welcome the New Year.

After shoving more logs into his large heater, Leclerc followed his wife and niece to bed, undressing quickly and scurrying under the covers. He had not quite fallen asleep when he heard noises outside that he later said sounded like "the mooing of cows". Wondering whose cattle could be wandering about on a night like this, he turned over and dozed off. He was soon jerked awake by his niece, Albertine Chavot, crying out, "Uncle, wake up! I hear someone hollering outside. You'd better get up and see!"

Hurriedly, Victor pulled on some clothes, asking himself what would bring anyone to his place on such a desperate night. Opening the door, he looked out and saw a blaze of fire, leaping high against the dark wintery sky to the north, the vicinity of the farm of his neighbor, Louis Bouchard. Then his gaze was pulled to the road where a figure was stumbling toward the house. He heard a man's voice cry out, "Victor! Victor, help me!" Running forward, Victor caught the man just before he fell.

In the dim light of the lantern he'd lit, he was able to recognize the man as Thomas Bouchard, who had arrived that fall to stay with his uncle, Louis Bouchard, and Louis' common-law wife, Annie Worotniak. Leclerc was stunned and horrified to note that Thomas was completely naked, with neither shoes nor clothes, wearing only a wristwatch.

With the help of his wife and niece, Victor carried Thomas into the house, wrapped him in blankets and put him to bed. "Thomas," Victor asked urgently. "What about your uncle and Annie? Are they coming behind you, or are they still in the house?"

He repeated the question several times before the dazed and half-conscious Thomas Bouchard was able to respond.

"Finished," he whimpered. "They're finished. I got my uncle outside once, but he's back in just the same." He added a few incoherent remarks about being wakened by the fire to find Annie on the floor and his uncle running around.

After hearing Thomas's story, the excited Leclerc rapped out to his niece: "Albertine, get dressed at once and run to Emard Champoux. Tell him to bring his tractor from his heated garage so he can drive Thomas to the hospital in Mclennan and let the Mounties know what happened. And on your way back stop at Blanchette's house and tell him to come and help us. Go quickly now!"

Leclerc then put on his boots, hat, and heavy coat and started toward the Bouchard place. From the size of the blaze he realized there was little hope he would find Louis or Annie alive. As he trotted through the loose snow, crossed the fence, and headed down the laneway toward the house, he wondered how the fire had started. He had visited Bouchard often and knew the pipes, stove connections, and chimney were all well protected against over-heating.

By the time Leclerc was close enough to hear the hissing and crackle of the flames, he could see the outbuildings had just started to catch fire. Fortunately the night was free of wind and Leclerc was able to prevent the fire's spread by throwing snow on the buildings. Then he reached the south side of the house. The heat was too intense for him to enter or even come near the doorway; however, he could detect what appeared to be a body, burnt beyond recognition, sprawled just inside the house beside the open door. Leclerc used a plank to scoop up snow and threw it on the corpse to douse the few flames still snaking along its outer edges.

Hoping to learn the fate of Annie, he moved around to the other side of the house; but the heat here was too much for him to get close enough to peer inside.

He turned and headed home, arriving just as Thomas was being carried out to Champoux's tractor for the twenty-mile trip to Mclennan. Shortly after, Blanchette, another neighbor, appeared on the scene and he and Victor made haste back to the fire with shovels. As they came within the light generated by the flames they saw that yet another neighbor, Joseph Lebrecque, had made his way across the fields to investigate the fire.

Although the blaze had subsided somewhat, it was still not possible to enter the house because of the heat and dense smoke. Leclerc pointed out the body, which had begun to burn again, and the men took turns shovelling snow on it until the flames were once more extinguished. They stayed around for a while longer. Then, deciding there was nothing more they could do that night, they made their way back to their respective homes.

Later that afternoon, a car pulled up bringing Corporal Fountain of Mclennan's RCMP detachment and Dr. Piche, acting as coroner, to the Leclerc home. At the policeman's request, the farmer hitched his team to a sled and drove the two officials to the scene of the fire. By now the fire had burned itself out and it was possible to move carefully through the rubble. John Worotniak, Annie's father, had already arrived on the scene and had pulled out two burned and unrecognizable bodies which were taken to Mclennan for identification and post-mortem examination.

As he helped load the blanket-shrouded bodies onto the sled, Victor Leclerc could only reflect that it was a tragic end for the sorry little man who had asked for so little from life and received even less. Why was he destined never to find the domestic happiness for which he'd searched so desperately?

Louis Bouchard had been only 18 when he married, in Chicoutimi County, a 15-year-old girl from his native Granby, Québec. At the time he had a fairly good job in a local plant and the young couple was able to purchase a small home. In the first year of their marriage a baby girl was born to them, but their happiness was short-lived. The child died and the young mother, unable to bear this crushing blow, began to see other men. Over the next few years there were many quarrels. The Bouchards separated and came together again at least six times, and in the process Bouchard lost a number of jobs and eventually his home. Finally he and wife went to court, although the outcome of the trial is unclear. At last the embittered man talked to his priest, who advised him to leave and seek a new life for himself.

For the next dozen years or so he wandered across the face of Canada, finding work wherever he could—in factories and bush camps, with farmers and railways, his travels taking him further and further west until he arrived in Girouxville in the Peace River country. It was one of a number of communities of Québec farmers, planned and settled by the Catholic Church in the early part of the century. Here Louis was able to find land. He built a small house and once again became part of society. Soon after he settled he visited the local priest, urging him to write to Québec to find out if his wife was still alive. He claimed that he visited the priest twice, but had no response that his wife still lived.

Louis wanted to remarry. Not hearing from the church that his first wife was still alive, he believed he was free to try again. For over a year he kept company with a local girl. But before they could marry, people from the Granby area whispered to the girl's mother that Louis already had a wife in Québec. The romance came to a quick end.

Some years later Louis tried again. The same rumor once again cropped up. This time the intended bride's sister took it upon herself to write to Québec for the facts and, in due course, received confirmation of his earlier marriage as well as a letter from his wife in which she enclosed a photo of herself and Louis. Armed with her proof, the woman drove to her brother's farm where Louis was helping with the harvest. There in front of the family and neighbors she read out the letters and passed around the photo. The wretched and humiliated Louis was warned to get off the land and never to try to see his intended bride again.

These misfortunes might well have cooled the zeal of most men. But not Louis Bouchard. He wanted a wife to cook for him and share his cabin and his bed. His first two marriage attempts had been with French-speaking girls whose families still had ties with the Québec homeland. Now, Louis went courting further afield, 20 miles to the north to the Lac Macgloire district where a number of central-European families, from Poland, Hungary, and the Ukraine, had settled. Here he met and quickly married Annie Worotniak, a girl less than half his age. But once again the people of Girouxville began to talk and it was not long before some good soul carried the tale to the RCMP. An investigation was launched, Louis was charged and sentenced to a year in the provincial jail for committing bigamy and he duly served his sentence. Upon his release he returned to his farm to live with Annie Worotniak as his common-law wife.

Meanwhile, Thomas Bouchard had been following his uncle's path, working his way slowly westward across Canada in mines, logging camps, on the railway and farms. In between had been a stint of military service. In 1946, arriving in Alberta, he decided to make for the Peace River country where he knew he had an uncle. By now in his late twenties, Thomas had grown weary of the vagabond life. He had saved some money and hoped his uncle might help him find land.

Thomas arrived in Edmonton in October and from there caught the Northern Alberta Railways passenger train north. He was an affable young man with an easy manner and on the overnight trip struck up an acquaintance with several farmers from the Girouxville area. Over drinks on the train that night the men decided to play a joke on Louis when they all got into Girouxville. The next morning Thomas awoke to a flat fertile land, sliding past his window. A few minutes later the train pulled up at the station with its small frame stationhouse and large grain elevators, already receiving truckloads of grain.

After breakfast and a few drinks at the hotel with his new friends, Thomas was driven to the Bouchard place by Arthur St. Laurent and another neighbor. St. Laurent solemnly introduced Thomas to Louis as a government agent sent to check registered cattle brands. "He has come particularly to see you, Louis. And now you must show him your papers." At this, Louis, whose experience with any level of government had not been pleasant, looked so alarmed that the men began to laugh.

The other neighbor cried out, "Don't worry, Louis. We're just having a joke. This is really your nephew, one of your family."

Louis still looked skeptical so the younger Bouchard broke in, "It's true, uncle. I'm the son of your brother, Joseph, and have been working in Alberta. My sisters wrote that my grandfather, your father, has just died and said I should come to tell you. So here I am."

His expression still glum, Louis grumbled, "I don't know why anyone would want to come to this land. It is a place of misery and has meant much hard work for me."

"But, Uncle, you have a good farm with a house, stock, and machinery. You're much better off than many back in Chicoutimi."

"Well, maybe you are right," the older man conceded, "bring your bag and Annie will fix you something to eat."

The others left and over their meal, uncle and nephew spoke of the family back east. Thomas said he was tired of wandering and wanted a farm of his own. "I have saved some money," he said. "Not enough to buy land as well as machinery, but my father will help me."

Louis showed Thomas his buildings and they walked over part of the land. After supper that night, Annie set up a cot in the small house and screened it for privacy.

In the beginning it was an amicable arrangement. Thomas helped with the chores and the fall farm work. At one time he even loaned his uncle money for a pressing debt. Once in a while they went to town, sometimes with Annie. There Thomas visited the friends he had met on the trail and through them met other members of the community. But the harmony was not to last.

The contrast between uncle and nephew was all too apparent to Annie. Thomas was young, tall, and nice-looking with an affable smile and outgoing manner, while Louis, bowed by the weight of his past experiences, with a wrinkled countenance, sparse hair, and a deliberateness of speech, seemed a great deal older than his years. Bored and restless, thrown into close contact with the visitor, Annie began showing an interest in Thomas and did not always bother to conceal her feelings.

Louis sulked and withdrew into his shell. Certainly the

cramped conditions of the little farmhouse did not make the situation any easier. As Christmas approached, tension built. Louis became even more gruff and uncommunicative. Small problems created bitter arguments. There was a long and stormy dispute between Annie and Louis over buying her a winter coat. When Thomas offered to pay for the coat, the quarrel became even more violent. One day Thomas was presented with a new scarf. When he tried to thank his uncle, Louis said bitterly, "Don't bother to thank me. It's not my present. She gave it to you." And he stamped from the house.

Now it must be understood that Thomas, as the sole survivor, is the only source of information about what did take place in the Bouchard household. Naturally, he would not be a completely unbiased witness. He always maintained it was the girl who came after him, that he made no advances, and that he told her to stay away from him. According to him, she once asked, with obvious meaning, "I want you to do something for me. Will you?" He told her he would not and left the house. Later, he claimed, Annie asked him outright to come to bed with her, but he shook his head and again left the house.

His story may well be true and, if so, casts the young man in a temperate and decent role. Yet the uncle was certain the two young people were taking advantage of him and his conduct shows he tried to catch them out. More than once he would make an excuse to leave the house, then sneak back. Thomas, alarmed, again warned Annie to stay away.

Monday, December 30, Louis said he was going to Mclennan with Victor Leclerc to buy some liquor for a party he planned for friends and neighbors. He returned earlier than was expected and Thomas felt sure he had been hanging around outside the house for some time before coming in. Later, as Annie was curling her hair, Louis sneered: "You must think you're a princess. You act as if you are far too good to work around here." And he slammed out of the house.

In the afternoon the two men went out to do the chores. According to Thomas, they worked in deadly silence. Thomas retired to bed early and from where he lay on his cot, he could hear Louis and Annie talking in low voices. He could not hear what was said except once when Louis broke out in a loud and angry voice, "It will not go on like this much longer!"

When he awakened the next morning, New Year's Eve, Thomas again heard Louis talking to Annie in a rough voice. He offered to do the morning chores himself, but Louis curtly told him they would share the work. Later the older man hitched his team to the sled and drove to the Leclerc farm to fetch the liquor he had bought the day before. Returning home he began to drink, mixing beer with rum and homemade wine. He continued to drink heavily through the afternoon and into the evening after the chores were done.

Whatever the senior Bouchard had said to Annie apparently had no effect on her. As Thomas recounted, "She kept coming after me. I tried to ignore her and started a conversation with my uncle which he just disregarded." It was not a very pleasant way to spend New Year's Eve, so, after listening to the French radio station, Thomas went to bed around 9:30 p.m. Because of the cold, he left on his long underwear; it could get pretty bad in the house once the fires had died and the radio had promised even lower temperatures by morning.

As he moved behind the curtains to crawl into bed, he could see his uncle still at the table pouring himself large drinks, mixing the beer with the rum and wine. Annie sat at the table with him, although she was not drinking. Every so often she made a sharp rejoinder to Louis, who kept mumbling and growling at her.

According to the first statement Thomas gave the police, he fell asleep quickly and was awakened to a great shout. Annie called out his name several times. He peered out from between his curtains and was surprised that the inside of the cabin was very bright, far different from the dull flicker which came from the house lantern. He looked up to see his uncle standing over him before feeling a heavy blow to his head and falling unconscious to the floor. When he came to he felt strong blasts of cold air blowing on him from the open door. His uncle was now near the stove, and pouring gasoline from a five-gallon can onto the floor. Thomas saw now that the bright light was a fire burning inside the house, and Annie was lying face down near the stove.

As Thomas staggered to his feet, Louis turned and started toward him, but the younger man was able to push him back. Louis retreated toward the open door, then stooped to pick up a heavy object which he hurled at his nephew. Thomas ducked, and there was a crash of glass behind him. By then the fire was, in Thomas' own words, "beginning to jump," and Louis dashed out into the yard. Thomas followed and the two men struggled. Louis broke away and they fought again further out in the yard. Louis picked up a stick of firewood and swung it at his opponent. Thomas was able to wrest it away, then struck the older man with it several times until Louis fell to the snow. Thomas now noticed that his uncle's pant leg was burning where gasoline had splashed on it. He leaned over to examine him; later he claimed he was positive he was dead.

Thomas then ran back to the house. The fire had spread and was leaping high. Annie's body on the floor was now aflame but the heat was too intense for Thomas to enter. Returning to where Louis lay, he dragged his uncle to the doorway and, after two attempts to come close enough, finally managed to heave the body into the house. Spotting a can of coal oil by the door he also tossed it into the blazing house and heard the stove "go boom."

It was then he noticed blood on his underwear, so he peeled it off and threw it in as well. Suddenly aware of the bitter cold he turned and ran toward the Leclerc house.

Bouchard's frostbite kept him for some time in the Mclennan hospital where some of his toes were amputated. He was lucky in view of his mad dash, completely naked, over a distance of almost a mile in minus 40 degree weather, to escape with such minor damage.

Nevertheless, while in hospital, Thomas Bouchard was charged with the murder of his uncle, Louis Bouchard. The community reacted with shock and disbelief. Although he had lived in the district only a few months Thomas Bouchard was well thought of and had made many friends. Most people simply would not accept the police version that he had actually killed his uncle outside the house, then thrown his body into the blaze. From the fragmented and garbled sentences Thomas had mumbled in shock and hysteria, and in intense pain from frozen feet, Victor Leclerc thought Thomas had tried to rescue Annie and his uncle from the burning house and had run naked to get help. Word spread quickly through the community. Thomas was believed to be a hero.

This was one of those murders where the defendant is the sole survivor and there is no other direct evidence, either oral or written. In such cases, the prosecution's game is to somehow make the person labelled as the culprit give statements which will establish guilt. But this must be done within the limits established by the criminal code. In other words, such statements must be proven to be voluntary. Now, most people would think that only a fool would admit guilt, or facts from which guilt could be inferred, particularly after being told by a kindly policeman that he or she does not have to say a word. But, illogical as it may seem, a great many are convicted out of their own words. Policeman aren't always kindly and there have been many cases when it was unclear if police warnings were properly and legally given. More important is the mental condition of the person in custody who often has an overpowering urge to talk to someone... anyone. Well-trained police officers are aware that at a certain point, words will come gushing out.

Thomas Bouchard wanted to talk. He made his first rambling comments at the Leclerc house. Later, he made a lengthy statement to Corporal Fountain, the French-speaking noncommissioned officer stationed at Mclennan. This was put into writing and Bouchard signed it. He gave further statements to police officers on guard at the hospital. He was also interviewed by Sergeant Guimond, an experienced senior, French-speaking officer. He was especially detailed to the case from the Lethbridge staff of the RCMP. The series of interviews, spread over a three-day period, produced a lengthy document, much of it the product of questioning. When the case came to trial, the defence strongly attacked it for this reason. A few days later, Bouchard asked for pen and paper and wrote a letter to his father, setting out an account of what had happened. The authorities seized it, then produced it at his trial for evidence.

There were substantial variations on a number of details in Thomas's statements. Yet many of the major elements of his story remained the same in all his written and oral statements and letters—Louis Bouchard's sullen attitude; his harassment of Annie; his drinking; and Thomas's awakening to find the cabin aflame and Annie on the floor and his uncle now attacking him.

When his case came before a jury, much would depend on what statements would be allowed to be put in evidence and the skill in advocacy the opposing counsel would use in dealing with them. My own experience in the practice of criminal law has persuaded me to the theory that once an accused has opened the gate by making a statement, the basics of what was said will be repeated in all subsequent conversations and confessions, just as a wound-up toy monkey on a stick will go through a set performance. So it is imperative to study with great care the details of the entire package in order to arrive as near as possible to the truth.

When the police were finished with Bouchard, and his injuries had healed to the point where he could travel, he was bundled onto a train and sent out to the provincial jail at Edmonton to await a preliminary hearing and then a supreme court jury trial. The preliminary was held in Mclennan on April 9, with Magistrate William Stewart presiding and Sandy Phimester, the attorney general's Peace River agent, conducting the case for the prosecution.

With the same penurious attitude that marked the conduct of the department of the attorney-general in those days, the accused was not represented by counsel, but was entirely on his own. Of course, there was very little cross-examination and no real opportunity to challenge the Crown witnesses. Not only that, but the Mclennan trial was conducted mainly in English, although there was an interpreter for witnesses who asked for such assistance. Thomas Bouchard had picked up some knowledge of English in the course of his wanderings across the country, but he was not proficient. Further, he lacked any understanding of the legal terms used and the medical evidence presented by doctors. He thought, spoke, and wrote primarily in French. So he was at a considerable disadvantage, which is easily shown by the transcript of the proceedings.

I know many will say, "So what? The fellow was guilty of wrongdoing, so why help him out?" But guilty of what specific offence? What are the relevant facts? Are there mitigating circumstances? And if found guilty, what is the sentence to be? What is at risk under these conditions is not just the fate and future of one individual, but of an entire system, the need to preserve a delicate balance between a person and the enormous power of the state. The power of those involved in law enforcement often leads to their confusing the means with the end. The system, if well and carefully used, even with all its faults and man-made abnormalities, must still enable the facts to be ferreted out by trial, hearing witnesses, listening to argument, and allowing a jury to declare what those facts are. All this so that in our democratic institutions, justice can be done, and be seen to be done, by and for those who are part of it; a far better situation than that prevailing in most of the world today, where the truth is whatever the authorities declare it to be.

It was a foregone conclusion that Thomas Bouchard would be committed to stand trial at the next competent sitting of the supreme court to be held at Peace River for the murder of his uncle, Louis Bouchard. Once committed, he was not given a chance to be released on bail, but was despatched to Edmonton to await his rendezvous with judge and jury. Because his money had been destroyed in the fire, he was without funds to engage counsel on his own and had to await the largesse of the government. In due course my father's firm in Peace River was appointed to undertake the defence. I had only just been discharged from the army within the past year and was living in Edmonton at the time. But I'd heard of the case and during my few trips north kept track of what was going on through my old firm and friends.

Bouchard's Peace River trial took place on June 23, 1946, with Mr. Justice Campbell McLaurin presiding. Jury selection went smoothly. One juryman did have a knowledge of the French language, which was probably a plus for the accused.

The trial lasted the best part of two days and focused almost exclusively on the major questions of the so-called confessions to the police and the letter written to his father by the accused, particularly the admission of the killing and the placing of the body in the fire. Equally, the defence emphasized the attack on Annie, the heavy drinking, and the crucial point where Louis had attempted to kill Thomas just after starting the fire. As well, supplementary and explanatory testimony was given. There was evidence from the first doctor on the scene, from some neighbors and, of course, from the police, who retained or identified certain exhibits. Hair and blood stains had been found outside, as well as the piece of firewood alleged to have been used as a weapon. False teeth, photos of the inside and exterior of the burned building and, of course, the usual gruesome photographs of the charred and blackened bodies of Louis Bouchard and Anne Worotniak, were introduced.

This is a favorite move in any prosecution—to take many pictures of the murder scene and submit in evidence the most bloodcurdling of them, irrespective of their relevance.

Most importantly, the long statement taken by Sergeant Guimond of the Lethbridge RCMP was excluded, mainly on the grounds that surrounding circumstances suggested it did not completely meet the test of being voluntary. Also ruled out was the letter the young man had written to his father. The other statements were admitted in evidence and these, including Bouchard's explanations and comments, came before the jury.

There was then evidence that Louis Bouchard came to his death as a result of blows struck by his nephew. But this evidence also showed a picture of suspicion, jealousy, and anger, of an older man who believed his young common-law wife was infatuated, and likely sleeping with a younger man; a story of heavy drinking and wild actions, all bottled up within the close quarters of a tiny shack, and then an eruption of violence, killing, and burning, started by the older man and finished by Thomas.

The judge took the best possible explanation from the viewpoint of the defence, and, in his directions to the jury, pointed out that a verdict of not guilty could be supported by the evidence. He had to couple this with reference to other possible verdicts of manslaughter and murder. He did tell the jury they were the sole judges of the facts.

After the jury retired, Crown counsel took exception to the charge. Following a brisk argument, the judge recalled the jury and placed more emphasis on the case for manslaughter. And it was manslaughter which the jury brought in as a verdict. The accused had admitted striking the blows which killed Louis Bouchard, and that he had placed his uncle's body in the burning building. It just went against the grain of the jury to say Thomas was home-free on everything and turn him loose.

This sort of thinking is irrelevant in strictly legal terms; if Louis was dead when dragged into the shack, it could not affect the manner of his killing. Nevertheless, Thomas's action had deeply offended the jury's sense of propriety. I was also told that Thomas's action in trying to destroy the body was felt by some to be the conduct of a man with a guilty mind.

Possibly. But don't forget this activity, this violence and bloodshed, was the culmination of an intense, highly-emotional, wildly physical few minutes. Those who frame the criminal code, sitting in their snug offices, talk of a standard of "reasonable people," as being the measure by which ordinary people must conduct themselves. Ask a soldier who has been in combat, or ask a policeman on patrol in a crime-infested district about this standard of "reasonable people," and you'll get a blank look.

Collectively the jury, mixing law with common sense, had reached an adequate decision.

In any event, the sentence was light—three years—which, with good conduct, would bring Thomas Bouchard back to society in a reasonably short time.

CHAPTER SEVEN

The Wife Who Fought Back

THE CASE OF FLORA GLADUE, CHARGED WITH THE death of her husband, John Gladue at Atikameg, a tiny native settlement, was directly related to the use of alcohol. The year was 1952.

The issue of alcohol abuse by native people is one which cannot be avoided, although for many years those in authority have attempted to sweep it under the rug. Some of the blame rests on traders and land agents, who attempted to get their hands on furs and land script with rum, whiskey, and rotgut homebrew. But let there be no doubt governments over the last several generations have to assume much of the blame also. It is a running sore in the history of Canada.

Most treaties between Ottawa and native tribes were entered into to enable the Dominion government to dispose of western lands and resources and to quieten the titles of those who acquired the lands. However, there were other provisions, and common to many was one whereby the government undertook to keep liquor away from the Indians. The government agencies were not solely responsible for having these clauses inserted. Many older native leaders, alarmed at the excessive use of alcohol by their people and the damage created, clamored to have treaties written accordingly. As a result, there were heavy penalties for selling or giving liquor to natives covered by the act, status or treaty Indians. On the other hand, Indians who had relinquished their native rights were free to drink. It was a ridiculous ruling, full of anomalies. For 60 or 70 years it only created problems for those involved in the administration of the law and criminal justice. I was co-chairman of a joint parliamentary committee in 1960—61 responsible for reviewing the terms of the Indian Act. Nothing gave us more concern than this issue. Not until the 1960s was this interdiction removed from the Act.

An inevitable result was that many native people, having a low tolerance to alcohol, were very likely to become easily intoxicated and out of control when they did get hold of liquor. From this unhappy circumstance came many violent incidents. Those of us involved in the law in the north were well aware of this. It was always a factor to be taken into account. Deny alcohol to some native people but allow others who live nearby to drink, and there you have a recipe for danger and confusion—a classic Catch-22 situation if there ever was one.

The case of Flora Gladue is an apt illustration of the tragedies and heartaches suffered by native people in their struggle to pull out of the swamp of misery into which the neglect and bad faith of governments had driven them.

Flora was a product of the mission school system. She had attended the Anglican school at Wabasca, a small centre some miles to the east of her village. There were several church schools with good teachers and student dormitories at Wabasca. Flora had been a bright and alert student, liked by her classmates as well as her teachers. She had graduated from high school with good marks, and was so well regarded by the staff that a few weeks after the story of her case broke in the press, I had a letter from the former principal of her school, expressing shock that Flora had been charged with the murder of her husband. The teacher wrote of her in most glowing terms. He described her school record, and offered to travel to Peace River at his own expense from southern Alberta to give testimony on her behalf at her trial. Flora's husband, John, had also gone to the same school. He, too, had been rated a good, hard-working student.

Today, both of these young people are the sort who might have gone to university or, at least, to a technical school. Thirty-five years ago they did not have a chance. In those years only a pitifully small number moved beyond high school, sometimes through exceptional tenacity and brilliance, sometimes through luck in finding a sponsor. The rest returned to their small villages and bush camps. There, they often experienced a terrible letdown. There was little challenge for the talents and learning they had acquired in school. They had learned of another world to which they were now denied access.

This was the story of the Gladues.

After their marriage, Flora and John Gladue established a home in Atikameg, a seasonal trapping and fishing village north of Lesser Slave Lake. There was a chance to eke out a few extra dollars from hunting, but there was no industry, very little social life, and not much money. By 1952, the Gladues had six children. John made a living of sorts from fishing, hunting, and trapping. He drank a lot, and his need to get drink raised other problems.

In this part of the country, treaty and non-status native people live side by side. Although the sale of liquor and the issuing of beer licenses were under the control of the provincial government, the understanding with the federal government was that the province denied alcohol sale licenses within the immediate vicinity of any treaty Indian reserve. It was many miles from Atikameg to the nearest government liquor store or licensed beer parlor. As a result, many natives, treaty and non-treaty, made their own. Much of it was pretty awful, even dangerous. ''Moose milk'' was the name used to describe the concoction. It was usually made in large batches.

The Gladues were expert moonshiners, particularly John. After all, he was a heavy drinker with no place to buy whiskey and no money to buy it with. Unfortunately, when John drank, he was almost always ugly and abusive. Flora, his wife, invariably suffered from what he said or did. The very day John died, there was a freshly made batch of moose milk within the Gladue house.

I first met Flora Gladue in the interview room of Peace River's RCMP subdivision a short time after her arrest on the charge of killing her husband. She was a slender young woman in her late twenties, guarded and not too communicative at first. In truth, she responded only briefly to my direct questions. I was about to tell her I could not help her unless she was more open and frank, when I realized she was still in a state of shock and depression. I broke off our interview after telling her she had friends who wanted to help and they had asked me to tell her this. I also told her that her children were well and were being taken care of.

It was several days before she was able to throw off her depression. During our subsequent meetings I found her alert, intelligent, and willing to actively co-operate in her defence. About two weeks later I managed to get out to Atikameg. It was located some 75 miles northeast of High Prairie, and to get there I travelled from High Prairie by car and then by wagon through Grouard, along the winding bush trail to the little village.

All that was Atikameg was a few cabins, a small elementary school, a trading post, and a little mission, all straggled along a few dusty trails, lanes rather than roads. Along the lake's edge, I saw some boats, and hungry-looking dogs skulked around the shacks.

The able-bodied men fished and hunted for food and worked trap lines for pitifully small amounts of cash. With some welfare and family allowance, that gave them just enough to buy basic essentials. There was almost no recreational outlet except for intermittent drinking. The Gladues led a sorry and bedraggled existence in Atikameg. So did many others.

The last drinking party at the Gladue home had been several weeks before, on May 10, 1952. Both of them and some of their friends had drunk an immoderate amount of homebrew. During the party, John had beaten his wife, cuffing her around and knocking her down. Flora defended herself within the limits of her strength. Her husband was stocky and muscular, weighing over 170 pounds and used to an outdoor life, and I doubt if she tipped the scales at more than 120 pounds.

Just before May 10, John returned from spring trapping in the bush with a little money. As soon as he arrived home, he gathered his materials and made a batch of homebrew. Flora helped him. It must have been a big operation because the results were two containers, each holding two gallons of moose milk. The mixture was a raw, potent, nerve-twisting intoxicant. It had an immediate and overpowering effect. We were able to determine that John, with some help from Flora, drank nearly two gallons that fatal day.

Flora's sister, Jean Laboucan, was in the Gladue home most of the day. Apart from Flora, she was the only adult witness to the events leading up to the killing. Jean was 19 and lived with relatives in the hamlet, but she spent a great deal of time at her sister's to help with the children. Although Jean's English was adequate, and I had no trouble understanding her, she preferred to talk in Cree through an interpreter.

This was a common practice in those times among natives involved in legal proceedings. I think it was a comfort to a native witness, particularly one in the higher courts. Moreover, talking through an interpreter, a person has time to consider the question and frame an answer—usually as brief as possible—and be less likely to get into difficulties. On the other hand, this could be exasperating for an examiner. If he had discussed a situation previously in English with a potential witness, it was not helpful to discover a day or two later the same person now needed an interpreter and was unsure what had taken place. Cross-examining native witnesses required unlimited patience and a soft tongue.

The sudden death of John Gladue and the arrest of Flora made those living in the community even more reticent than usual in talking to the authorities. There was a natural urge not to say or do anything to cause Flora more harm. Even though the residents knew I was on Flora's side, by the time I arrived at Atikameg, the authorities had already been there—police, doctors, other officials—and some were still around. So answers to my questions were more terse and monosyllabic than usual. In particular, if Mounties were in the vicinity, and they were, it was extremely difficult for any outsider, myself included, to obtain frank and open statements.

I was at least fortunate to talk to Jean Laboucan, Flora's sister, with the help of a sympathetic interpreter, "Big Joe" Cardinal. Luckily, too, because the girl had not yet been subpoenaed as a Crown witness, she was at liberty to talk freely to me. When she appeared on the witness stand at both the preliminary hearing and the trial, I had a fair idea what her evidence would be.

Jean lived at the house of her aunt, Nelly Laboucan, about a fifteen-minute walk from the Gladue place. She came every day to help Flora around the house. The youngest of the six Gladue children was two, and Flora had her hands full. Having stayed with Flora and John before moving to her aunt's, Jean had a pretty good idea what the situation was between the husband and wife. Jean was a bright and alert young woman. Once she adjusted to the strange environment of the courtroom and its procedures, she was most helpful.

According to Jean's story, she had arrived at the Gladue cabin around 10:00 a.m. May 10. She recalled the couple had been drinking intermittently, particularly John. By the time Jean arrived at the cabin, John had had a good start. Jean looked after the children, fed them, and prepared lunch for her sister, John, and his two brothers. They showed up in the early afternoon, but went home before supper. She fed the children their evening meal about 6:00 p.m. Then she helped Flora make supper for the adults. She told me Flora had not looked very well, had been quiet, and had stood off to one side while the meal was being prepared. John was drinking heavily, shouting, and cursing.

When supper was ready, John stopped drinking, came to the table, and began to eat. Flora would not take her place at the table, but remained standing across the room. It was still light at the time. John told her to come to the table, but she did not move.

When Flora did not come to the table, her husband shouted at her to sit down. Then he pushed back his chair, jumped from his seat, and began to beat her.

According to Jean, events during these drinking bouts always followed the same pattern: "When they get some money, John goes to get what they have to for the brew. They work together to mix it and would not wait too long before they started to drink. Others would come in and maybe there would be a party, and the party would last until the crocks were empty. At the end there would be fighting and yelling and arguing." It was at this stage that John would become belligerent and beat Flora up, then one or both would pass out.

On the afternoon of May 10, after Flora had been knocked down for the second time by her husband, hit in the face and around the head, she got to her feet and grabbed a piece of firewood. Jean took the stick away from her sister. She felt something terrible was going to happen. John returned to his meal. Jean turned to John, "Stop, John, leave her alone! Don't hit her anymore!"

There was no reply from John. After a moment, Flora turned, walked out of the house, and started down the trail. At this, the baby, awakened by the shouting and noise, began to cry. Jean went to the crib to comfort the child. Then John yelled and ran out of the cabin after his wife. Jean stayed in the cabin with the children, feeling she should not leave them, although she was afraid for her sister. Two of the older children did follow their parents from the cabin. A few minutes later, one came tearing back, screaming for Jean to come outside and see what had happened.

Jean ran from the house, down the track in the direction the Gladues had taken. There she found John, lying motionless by the side of the road. Flora was some distance off, heading toward the cabin of her aunt, Nellie Laboucan. John was dead, killed shortly before 7:00 p.m. by a blow from a stick in the hands of his wife, Flora.

Other than Flora, there were no observers; or, if there were, they did not come forward. One of the children had already run to tell Nellie Laboucan. He did not see anyone else in the vicinity. In any event, the child was too young to be sworn as a witness, nor competent to give testimony.

Jean, seeing that John seemed to be hurt quite badly, hastened to the Laboucan place, where she found her sister and told her, "You had better come back with me and see what you have done!" Flora, still holding the stick, seemed to be in a daze. She told her sister, "If I go back, I'll hit him again." Regardless, the two women returned to where John was lying on the road. Jean related that when Flora saw John she knelt down by him, took his hands, cried, "I didn't mean to kill him." Flora said that three times, according to Jean.

Another woman, John's sister, Florence Gladue joined them. They got water and bathed John's forehead. When he did not move, they were sure he was dead. With the help of some men John's body was moved to a nearby shack and Jean persuaded her sister to come back to her home where the children were waiting.

John's sister lived in a cabin along the road between her brother's home and the place where his body was found. Although she was watching from her window, she said she did not see the final struggle between the Gladues. She had noticed Flora hurrying by with a stick in her hand and she did see John break from a walk into a run after his wife. This was between 7:00 p.m. and 7:30 p.m. She did not bother to go outside and see what else was happening.

Big Joe Cardinal, who helped me question Jean Laboucan, was

a large man who lived in the Atikameg district. He spoke good English, was acquainted with the police, and was something of a leader in the community. After John Gladue was killed, he watched over the body the rest of the night. Some time around five in the morning, he saw Flora wandering in the bush alone. He called out to her, asking what had happened. She told him in Cree that she and John had fought, he had beaten her and knocked her down. She had run out of the house and he had come after her. When she looked back and saw him, she picked up a stick and started to run. Then he broke into a run. When John caught up to her, he hit her and held her head and was going to strike her again.

When I cross-examined Big Joe Cardinal, who gave evidence for the Crown, he recalled that Flora, telling her story to him, had used the words, "I hit at him with a stick so I couldn't get hurt again." Strictly speaking, this was hearsay evidence, but it was also part of the true issue. Her statement to Big Joe Cardinal, which he repeated at the trial, showed that she merely intended to defend herself.

I knew Cardinal well, having worked with him on other cases. Some years later he helped me during a political campaign in that part of the huge Peace River constituency. He was a friendly man and I always felt he could be depended on. Although he was a Crown witness, the overall impact of his evidence was tremendously helpful to us.

When the police arrived at Atikameg, they took Flora into custody. She made a brief statement to them before she was taken to Peace River and arraigned. There she made another statement which was put into writing. She was also questioned and freely gave replies. A man called Harry Lambert, who worked for the government and was himself part native, acted as interpreter and he assured me the woman appeared genuine and truthful. Flora's account of the struggle on the road with her husband was important because it was the pivotal issue of the legal effect of her actions.

The distance from where John's body was found to his house was fixed at about 300 yards. He had to be moving very quickly to catch her, particularly as she too was running. This suggests he was angry. The liquor had rendered him emotionally out of control, but he was still physically capable of doing considerable injury to her. This was obviously his intent. According to Flora's statement, John tried to grab her by the hair with one hand and hit her with the other. She had already been struck twice and knocked down inside their house. So she swung sideways with the stick to push his hands and arms away and free herself. She struck with a wide swing and hit him on the side of the head by his ear. She only struck him once. John dropped to the ground and Flora thought he was stunned.

After the stick was introduced as evidence by the court, I picked it up. At first sight, it was not a dangerous-appearing weapon, but it was actually very heavy. It had been in the lake at one time and become waterlogged. No doubt a crack with it to a sensitive part of the head could do considerable injury.

Another part of Flora's statement shed new light on the cause of the fight in the cabin. Flora said that John had demanded more butter for his meal. She brought it to him, but he was angry because she had not brought it to the table quickly enough. He threw it on the floor and shouted for her to pick it up. She did. Then he got up to beat her. I argued in court that John had deliberately tried to aggravate his wife so he could fight with her, then beat her.

The post-mortem examination was performed by Dr. J.B.T. Wood of the town of High Prairie. He testified death was caused by a cerebral hemorrhage resulting from a blow by a blunt instrument. He also felt such an injury was possible with one blow.

Lethal as the stick was, still it was obvious the young woman was running away and had simply picked up a stick lying in her path to defend herself.

The preliminary hearing was held at High Prairie, June 5, on a charge of murder before Mr. J.W. Bissell, the High Prairie magistrate. He committed Flora Gladue for trial at the next court of competent jurisdiction, which was to be held in Peace River, the following fall. Mr. Jack Shortreed, son of the Crown prosecutor in Edmonton, appeared for the Crown. He was eager to establish the foundation for a major charge of murder. Nevertheless, as the case progressed and the story unfolded from his own witnesses, it became obvious it would be manifestly impossible to make a murder charge stick. Shortreed himself must have come to this conclusion. Before he was halfway through putting in his case, he changed his line of questioning and, in fact, openly abandoned any attempt to establish a basis for murder. Rather he tried to lay a foundation for manslaughter, maintaining that although the accused had needed to defend herself, in doing so she had used more force than was necessary.

An arguable point, but to my mind it was destroyed by the look of one inanimate object—the stick. It was precisely the kind of object someone in distress would pick up to repel an assault. Guns and knives are offensive weapons; a stick, no.

A few weeks later, sure enough, I was advised that the attorney general had decided to proceed in the supreme court on an indictment for manslaughter against Flora Gladue. The murder charge had been dropped. This persuaded us to apply to a supreme court judge for an order releasing Flora on bail, pending her trial that fall in Peace River. Bail on capital murder cases is hardly ever granted. For manslaughter it is difficult, but not impossible. The order was granted. The facts related by witnesses at the preliminary inquiry had shown there was no likelihood this woman could or would leave the country, and there was need for her to look after her children. She could return home. This, of course, was another major breakthrough for us. It is a most solid psychological advantage in a homicide case for the accused to walk freely into court, rather than being brought in under police escort.

Court was held later that year at the Athabasca Anglican Church hall in Peace River. By now I felt very strongly that Flora Gladue was entitled to nothing less than a complete acquittal, but one of the main difficulties facing us was the meagerness of the evidence actually put on record at the earlier High Prairie trial. So little had been said, it would be hard to get at the issue.

Then there was the question of whether we still might want a jury trial now that the Crown had decided against a murder charge. The manslaughter charge made it a whole new ball game. An all-male jury, probably all married men, might take a dim view of a wife who had clubbed her husband to death. On the other hand, if the witnesses, who had already testified, said nothing worse than what was already contained in their High Prairie evidence, the defence would not be harmed. Further, the statement Flora had given and the evidence of Big Joe Cardinal both portrayed a woman fleeing from a man in a drunken rage. She had already been beaten. He had knocked her down that day, and he had a record of battering her whenever he drank his potent brew. She was entitled to be freed.

Nevertheless a jury is entitled to put its own interpretation of the facts into its verdict. If these men did go off on a tangent and find the accused guilty of manslaughter, Flora Gladue would go to jail for one or two years.

The judge coming up for the fall assizes was Ernie Wilson. He was a very good lawyer and a soldier with an excellent war record who had commanded the Edmonton regiment overseas. I regarded him as fair-minded, reasonable, and compassionate. Because I knew him to be a strong judge, I believed he would take the statement made by Flora Gladue in its entirety and not permit the Crown to place only what they wanted on record, putting aside the remainder.

After discussion with my client and some of her friends, we decided to do without a jury and allow Mr. Justice Wilson to try the case on his own. Still, our choice was not entirely free from doubt. By the time of the trial, Flora Gladue had been free on bail and back home with her children for two or three months, living in the community, and in day-to-day contact with witnesses who would be summoned by the Crown. I could not be sure what impact this would have on anyone's trial testimony.

The prosecution, in spite of its very strenuous efforts, was unable to produce any additional evidence. The original witnesses could not, or would not, say anything that made the Crown's case better. Early in its presentation, the Crown prosecutor called the RCMP officer and Harry Lambert, who had both been present when Flora gave her written statement. His Lordship carefully noted Flora's statement, particularly the last question and answer: "Did you swing the stick at John more than once?" "I didn't mean to hit him on the head. I meant to knock his hands away! I don't remember swinging the stick more than once."

When Big Joe Cardinal came to the stand later that day, I went over the same ground with him. He was as emphatic as he could be that the accused woman had told him the same thing when he spoke to her the morning after the killing. I stressed this point in my final argument to the court. I also dwelt on the nature of the weapon and the undisputed evidence that Flora had simply picked it up on the run.

When both counsel had completed the task of addressing the court, Mr. Justice Wilson made his own summary of the facts as established by the evidence. He concluded with a statement that a wife, attacked so brutally by her husband with the capacity and evidently the intent to cause her bodily harm, had every right to fight back and defend herself. He also found as a fact that Flora Gladue, the accused, had picked up the stick and swung it at her husband for the sole purpose of defending herself. Moreover, she was perfectly justified in doing so. Judge Wilson ended with, "I have no doubt the accused was endeavoring to avoid further punishment. The evidence as a whole leaves much doubt in my mind as to guilt." Then, turning to the young woman in the dock, he said, "Flora Gladue, stand up! I find you not guilty. You may go."

I had been watching her; her breathing was heavy, her eyes almost closed, her face taut. When the judge uttered his last words, she swayed a little, then turned slowly and walked through the crowd of silent, motionless spectators. She slipped out the door of the Athabasca hall, saying nothing to me or to any of her friends. When I left a few minutes later, she had vanished.

About two weeks later I received a warm letter from her. Flora Gladue apologized for her conduct and said although she had wanted to thank me and the people who had spoken for her, she had been in a daze. When the judge told her to go, she did just that, not knowing what she was doing. Not until she was home did she realize what had happened and then she felt dreadfully ashamed.

CHAPTER EIGHT

Testimony from the Grave

OUTSIDE IT WAS A GOLDEN, MELLOW DAY, THE KIND that makes the Peace River country so glorious in the early fall. But inside the small municipal hospital in the village of Fairview it was drab, sterile. The dark, narrow corridor leading to the wards from the reception area added to my feelings of unease. I stopped at the door indicated by the receptionist, knocked, and walked in. At first glance the small, narrow room seemed crowded to capacity, but I finally squirmed into a space beside my client, Mrs. Jenny Robertson. Seven people were in that room.

Lying on the bed was Ira Robertson, Jenny's husband. Under normal circumstances a thin spare man, today he was emaciated. The flesh had fallen from his face. His hands, inert, were like talons. The long outline of his body under the covers was skeletal. A mop of thick, dark, curly hair framed his head. His eyes were dark, large in the caverns of their sockets, brilliant in the intensity of the stare he directed at his wife.

It was Jenny who had fired the shot that had put him in the hospital with an injury to his spinal cord. He was now paralyzed from the waist down. Almost certainly, Ira Robertson was not going to survive the wound and he knew he was under a sentence of death.

Dr. O.J. McFadyen, the local medical doctor, had told Ira there was virtually no chance of his survival, with or without surgery. His condition was deteriorating daily and he would last no more than six months, if that.

What was taking place in the hospital that afternoon, September 14, 1937, was a preliminary inquiry (or part of a preliminary inquiry) into the attempted murder of Ira Robertson by his wife, Jenny Robertson, on September 2.

The law enforcement authorities had been keeping a close watch on Robertson's condition since the shooting, after which Jenny had been charged with attempted murder. Aware of the man's slim hold on life they kept her in custody, while awaiting his death so they could change the charge to one of murder. As a tactical move they decided to proceed at once with a preliminary hearing for attempted murder for the purpose of getting Robertson's evidence on the record. What they hoped to secure from the husband was some indication that Jenny had acted with deliberation, and not under a sudden impulse of fear, when she had gone upstairs to get a gun. However, her story had been confirmed by the only other eyewitness, Alice Burns. Thus, the process of the law had been set in motion and on September 14, a drab, dreary hospital room smelling of rotting flesh and heavy with the anticipation of death was just as much a courtroom as any large courthouse in the City of Edmonton, despite the lack of flag, coat-of-arms, or a picture of His Majesty.

If a person under expectation of imminent death, and believing this to be so, makes a statement, what is said can be received in evidence after the person has died. This is on the presumption that an individual expecting to die will not tell a lie. This gives a solemnity to the procedure and results in the willingness of the court to accept the declaration. Nevertheless, it was doubtful any statement Robertson made at this time could be received as a dying declaration because he was still hopeful of treatment to extend his time on earth, and the doctor had said he might live for several months. Moreover, there was some doubt that a statement made on a charge of attempted murder could be put forward on the entirely different charge of murder. However the authorities were very zealous to get a conviction and were prepared to plunge ahead.

I was the last character in the cast of this particularly grim drama and I took a quick look at the others. We were all sitting on narrow uncomfortable chairs, squeezed in between the bed with Robertson in it and the wall. William Stewart, the presiding magistrate, was a tall, heavy man and he sat at the head of the bed. Next to him was Corporal Lowes who was conducting the prosecution. Then came Dr. McFadyen who was present to keep an eye on his patient.

I was next and beside me was Jenny Robertson. A reporter was there to take down the statement, and finally there was Corporal Walker, Fairview RCMP.

Jenny had surrendered to Walker, a respected and first-rate policeman, when she met him while walking into Fairview immediately after she had shot her husband. Walker had been recruited from the Crow's Nest Pass district in the southern foothills of Alberta west of Lethbridge where rum-running and bootlegging were flourishing industries located only a few miles from the United States border. Walker's experience in this area of law enforcement had been one reason for posting him to Fairview.

The manufacture and sale of illegal liquor was a very profitable business in the Peace River area because for the past few years there had been a great increase in rail and road construction in the north country. This meant many construction camps and large numbers of workers. There were only two widely separated, legal liquor outlets in the whole of the region, Grande Prairie and Peace River. Walker had staged a spectacularly successful campaign against the professional bootleggers and operators, but he did not harass people who were only brewing from time to time a small batch of illegal whiskey for themselves or their friends. Consequently, local people did not hinder his efforts to stamp out the major sources of moonshine.

In my thinking "Curly" Walker was a good policeman in yet another sense. He never abused his position of authority or tried to worsen the situation of people involved in serious offences. He did not try to take advantage of them. He simply advised people of their rights. In giving evidence, he did not color his testimony in favor of the Crown.

The Robertson case was the first of three domestic tragedies—husband or wife killings—that took place during the last four months of 1937 in the Peace country. Each led to the spouse standing in the dock to face a murder charge and a possible death sentence.

The scene of the Robertson shooting was a farm about two-and-a-half miles south of the village of Whitelaw on the main highway between Peace River and Grande Prairie. On that farm was a frame house, not too far from the highway, and thinly screened by poplar trees. Although the Robertsons were childless, a fifteen-year-old girl named Alice Burns lived with them and called them "mother and father." She was reputed to be Jenny's niece. An eight-year-old boy also lived with them.

For several years the Robertsons' domestic life had been marred by incidents. Robertson had been charged at least three times with assaulting his wife. At the time of the shooting he was still bound over to keep the peace as the result of the last charge. As well, there had been civil proceedings and the two were legally separated. Although Ira resided at the farm during the fall and summer, they were living separately. The husband slept in an outbuilding and came to the house only for meals. Most definitely, they were not living together as husband and wife. I had acted for Jenny in several of these domestic tangles. I knew them both, had been in their home. A few days after Jenny's arrest I received a message to see her. I did so and was retained as her counsel.

The backgrounds of these two people were about as dissimilar in every way as could be imagined. I believe Jenny came to Canada from the southwestern United States, probably New Mexico, and was of Pueblo Indian ancestry. She was of less than average height, broadly built, almost squat, and not so much fat as well-muscled. Her countenance was brown, dark brown, her features almost always in repose, rarely showing emotion. Not an easy conversationalist, she spoke in short, simple words in a soft and rather pleasing voice. Ira, on the other hand, had been born in Scotland, emigrating to Canada as a young man. The many years spent in this country had not brushed away the burr and rasp of his native accent. He was of a man of ugly temper and rough language, tall and thin, with a narrow face and black curly hair that looked as if it was never brushed.

I never had the complete story as to how and why they came together; but I suspect Ira was a landless man who badly wanted his own farm and Jenny had the land, a house, and some money. Regardless, it was not long before they fell out and practically all the fighting grew out of the question of the land—its ownership and operation. Ira took the view that as husband he should control the farm and handle the money and business. At first Jenny agreed until she found he was squandering money on poor deals and mixing in bad company. She attempted to reassert her ownership. Out of this grew the fighting, the assault cases and, finally, the separation.

The summer of 1937 Ira had been hanging out with a man called Eddy Dodge who lived just a few miles to the west. According to Jenny, Dodge was responsible for much of the recent trouble between her and Ira. Although Jenny had put up the money for the seed and farming costs for the 1937 season, Ira was doing the actual work and was planning to take off the crop. Near the end of August Dodge had come to the farm and started an argument with Jenny over a piece of machinery he claimed Ira had given him permission to borrow. Jenny ordered Dodge off the land, telling him the machinery belonged to her, not Ira. Dodge used some filthy language and said, "You may not have too long to stay on this property. Anyway, Ira is around and I don't really have to go if I don't want to." Jenny still insisted he leave and this was the cause of another run-in with Ira.

It took several meetings with my client for me to get this and other relevant information from her. Her responses to my questions were terse and made in such a low voice, it was often difficult to follow the thread of her narrative. She hesitated frequently and often reversed or changed her statements, not so much because she was untruthful as because she was uncertain of the words to use to cover the facts. After checking her statements, I found they were in line with those she made to the authorities directly after her arrest. Nevertheless, from a technical point of view, I realized she would make a terrible witness.

According to Jenny, on the evening of September 1, 1937, just a day or so after the last run-in with Eddy Dodge, Ira came to the house and told her he was planning to hire two boys to help with the grain crop which he would be cutting soon. He added, "You'll have to arrange to feed them and put them up." Jenny answered, "There's not enough groceries in the house for two extra people. You've got money. You go get the supplies we need."

Ira blew up. "That's your job. That's for you to do. You get to town and bring back what we need!" When she refused, he blustered at her, "Mind what I say! Get the groceries or it'll be too bad for you!" He left the house, but a short time later returned for supper. Once again he began to abuse her, this time making a rush at her. The young girl, Alice Burns, stepped in front of her aunt to protect her. Cursing, Ira left with the threat, "I'll get rid of you yet!" Jenny went upstairs and came down with a .22 repeating rifle and followed Ira outside. There was a tussle and he grabbed the weapon from her, but she managed to recover it, taking it back to the house and stowing it in a trunk in her bedroom.

The next morning Ira came to the house from the bunkhouse where he slept. He took up the quarrel in the dining room as the family sat down to breakfast. The groceries for the helpers was merely a surface issue. What was really burning Ira was the land. It was her property, in her name, and he was there only by her permission. Ira began to taunt Jenny. "You won't be able to pay the taxes and the land will go up for sale, and I'll be able to buy it over your head." She answered that the land would never be his and, enraged, he swore and threatened her once more.

According to Alice Burns the fighting over the property had been growing worse. Ira had threatened Jenny with a razor and told her he would see her nailed in a wooden box. On another occasion Jenny had fired two warning shots into the roof. Then there was the last assault when he had beaten her and she had laid the charge against him. So it was an unhappy household, one that held the potential for tragedy. On the morning of September 2, 1937, that potential was realized.

Jenny left the table and climbed the stairs to her bedroom. Alice, who followed, saw her take the gun from the trunk and load it. Jenny looked frightened, but angry and determined. The girl descended ahead of her aunt and as she reached the stairwell saw Ira leave the table and scurry behind the partition at the bottom of the stairs, positioning himself so he could not be seen from the last few steps. Alice went immediately to the kitchen at the back of the house. She recalled later that as she left the room, Jenny had just reached the last step. A few minutes later Alice heard a shot and ran back from the kitchen to see Ira lying on the floor and Jenny standing over him, the rifle in her hands.

Jenny's version of the incident was the same as Alice's, except she added that when she reached the foot of the stairs, Ira sprang from behind the partition and started for her. It was then she fired at him.

Jenny Robertson was taken into custody and charged with attempted murder and, just twelve days later, the Crown staged its preliminary hearing with Ira Robertson examined as a witness, giving evidence from his bed in the Fairview hospital.

It was a difficult and unsettling experience for most of us present. Because of the man's condition I did not harass him with a cross-examination. I contented myself with his admission that he did not really recall the actual words or acts immediately before the shooting. This was a significant boon for the defence as he did not refute the version given by Jenny and corroborated by Alice.

The Crown had launched these early proceedings because they hoped Ira Robertson would produce positive and strong denials of Jenny's narrative. Corporal Lowes, who conducted the prosecution, was plainly disappointed at his failure to obtain an affirmation which could result in a successful capital prosecution. But he, too, hesitated to press the dying man too closely. The proceedings came to an abrupt end when Robertson was barely able to respond to further questions.

I walked to the door, then turned to hold it open for Jenny Robertson. As she rose to her feet, she raised her head and, for the first time since I had entered the room, looked directly at her husband. He met her gaze and I thought I saw a small smile play over his face. I might have been wrong. Maybe it was only the change of light from the open door. But I'd like to think otherwise!

Robertson died the afternoon of November 24. An autopsy was performed and two days later an inquest was held at Fairview to inquire into the cause of death. The evidence was much the same as that given at the earlier hearing except the results of the autopsy were presented. I was present only as an observer and did not request permission to examine any of the witnesses. However, I did obtain a copy of the proceedings and was particularly interested in the medical reports because directly following the shooting Jenny had sent Alice to the neighbors for help. She then walked the twelve miles to Fairview and turned herself in to the police. Before leaving she had hidden the rifle under some hay. A short time later a neighbor by the name of O'Neill arrived. He moved Ira Robertson to a mattress, turned him over to make him more comfortable and gave him water. Robertson was able to tell O'Neill he had some money and some grain checks and to give him their location. He also dictated a statement requesting that if he died, the money was to go to his brother in Scotland.

Dr. McFadyen and Corporal Walker were summoned from Fairview by telephone. They arrived and the doctor made a cursory examination. He noted the man's symptoms and Robertson was then rolled in a blanket and carried to a vehicle for transportation to the Fairview hospital.

After the inquest I spoke to some doctor friends and read up on the highly complex and technical subject of the vertebrae and spinal cord. Evidence given at the inquest concerning the way the wounded man had been moved by O'Neill and roughly bundled out to the truck made me wonder if this treatment might have exaggerated the damage done by the bullet. Could it even have made the wound fatal? Apparently so, as I learned over a year later in a casual conversation with an orthopedic surgeon, but I was able to get nowhere with the subject when I suggested the possibility during the trial.

Under normal circumstances Jenny Robertson's trial for an offence that took place at the beginning of September would have been held in Peace River at the fall assizes. However, because her husband did not die until the end of November this was not possible. Jenny would have been compelled to remain in jail until the next Peace River assizes, scheduled for June, 1938, if it had not been that hers was one of three domestic murder trials pending in 1937. A special sitting was proclaimed and gazetted. It is only in the rarest of circumstances that a person charged with murder is admitted to bail. I can recall a great many instances when men and women remained in custody for months on end awaiting their constitutional right of trial to determine their innocence or guilt. In our country the well-worn phrase "innocent until proven guilty" often loses its meaning when people are held for long periods under murder or manslaughter charges—or for other serious offences when bail is so large they can't possibly make it.

Jenny Robertson spent the Christmas of 1937 in jail in Edmonton, then was duly processed back to the north country. On Monday, January 17, 1938, I stood beside her as she faced Judge Tweedie to plead "not guilty" to the charge of murdering Ira Robertson and elect for trial by judge and jury. The jury was quickly selected and her case, the first on the docket, began the same day.

During the months Jenny was in prison I had interviewed a number of people in the district including neighbors whose names she had given me. Without exception they had all agreed that Ira Robertson had been a harsh and brutal man. For years he had subjected his wife to physical and verbal abuse. He had beaten her and continually battered her verbally. Because of my past association with Jenny as her solicitor I was already aware of this. I was reasonably sure that no northern jury would find her guilty of murder. Manslaughter was about all the Crown could hope for unless they had facts of which I was unaware. Or, unless Jenny Robertson on the witness stand convicted herself by her actions, manner, or words. I did not intend to allow this.

The trial followed a predictable course. The domestic discord between husband and wife was not at issue. The previous wife-beating charges against Ira and the separation were a matter of record. There was no denial there had been angry words between husband and wife the day before the shooting and the moment in time just preceding it. I did not get very far when I suggested Robertson might have sustained additional injury from the rough handling just after he was shot. However, the jury did note this point. Another bit of information which made them sit up was O'Neill's evidence that Robertson had been in possession of several hundred dollars yet had been so niggardly as to refuse to buy groceries for the men who worked for him. I argued before the jury that Ira had baited his wife for some time deliberately.

The Crown prosecuting team tried to make something of Ira's death bed statement, literally testimony from the grave. But in the context of the other evidence, it was not very strong stuff. I made no solid objection to the admission of this evidence, although there were substantial legal reasons for not allowing it. It has been my experience that, for appearance's sake, it is usually better not to request the exclusion of evidence which is not truly compromising.

The Crown had to content itself with insisting Jenny Robertson had acted on a premeditated course when she went upstairs for the rifle, then loaded it. The fine line between premeditation and reaction can mean the difference between a murder and a manslaughter conviction in cases like this. The Crown's approach, however, came to nothing in the face of Alice Burn's testimony. The girl gave her evidence in an open and straightforward manner. She looked the judge straight in the eye. It was difficult not to believe her when she stated, "Dad said he would see mother nailed in a coffin. That morning, after she said she would not let the land be sold for taxes, he made a run at her, and I had to get in between to protect her." Moreover, the Crown could not argue Jenny lied when she claimed Ira came from behind the partition and rushed toward her.

After counsel made their addresses, the judge, summing up, called for a manslaughter verdict. The jury brought in a verdict for manslaughter with "a very strong recommendation for mercy." Jenny Robertson was sentenced to three years in prison. However, time was allowed for the period she already spent in custody awaiting trial. My client was free in a little over a year. She did not return to the north.

CHAPTER NINE

Death at a Tea Party

IT HAS BEEN SAID MANY TIMES THAT TRUTH IS THE FIRST casualty in time of war. I would add that truth has become a basket case in the peace separating wars. All too often fact and fantasy seem interchangeable products in our enlightened age of information technology. To arrive at the truth so justice can be done in our society is not easy, nor in some instances does justice appear to be the objective.

Some time ago I attended a regional meeting of the American Bar Association in Los Angeles. At one session a judge of the Los Angeles Superior Court told of meeting a former colleague who came hurrying into the courthouse as the judge was leaving. Said the judge in a jocular manner, "Well, Billy, have you come here seeking justice?"

"Hell, no," came the reply, "I want to win one for a change."

Amusing as the story is, it cuts close to the nerve.

In the north in my time, the Crown was well equipped to get at the facts when they wanted them. They had the wide network of RCMP investigation and the local police to act as "go-fers." The Crown also had access to government files from both foreign and domestic agencies. They had all the funds they needed and could get as many experts in various fields as they asked for. Those of us who conducted criminal defences did not have those advantages, yet we were often able to prevent injustice being done. Let me tell you about the murder trial of Louis Napio.

Napio was a treaty Indian from the Calais trading post in northern Alberta. His father, a member of the band that lived, fished, hunted, and trapped around Sturgeon Lake, was a medicine man—one "who had the medicine." Despite conversion to

Christianity, many Indians retained belief in the wise man who, with his other skills, had the ability to peer into the future.

Louis Napio was known to be a man who could get up a good head of steam with very few drinks because several years earlier he had suffered a head injury and a small metal plate had been inserted in his skull. The pressure of the plate made him less tolerant to liquor. Under the Indian Act of the day, Napio could not be given alcohol by anyone; nor could he buy it. In fact, anyone giving or selling liquor to a treaty Indian was running counter to the law and liable to a heavy penalty.

One day in the early 1950s Napio and his wife, Mary, drove their wagon to a party given by a Métis family by the name of Ghostkeeper. The gathering was held in a cabin near Lake Winagami, about seven miles east of the railway center of McLennan. It was quite a party. Before it was over a man had been shot to death. Three days later Louis Napio was arrested at his father's home in Calais and charged with murder.

I entered the picture some weeks later when Louis Napio's father, John Napio, came to my Peace River office and requested me to undertake his son's defence. I had read about the case and taken it for granted the federal Indian Affairs Department would retain counsel. As a Liberal government was in power, it would be a lawyer with connections to that party . . . who was certainly unlikely to be me. Strangely enough, however, nothing had been done on Napio's behalf. Although a preliminary hearing and inquest had been held before a provincial magistrate, no one had represented Napio at either of these hearings.

This was a sad state of affairs. It is during the earlier hearings that the Crown first discloses its case. Any lawyer worth his salt can test then the story of witnesses and likelihood of the picture being painted by the Crown. It is also tremendously important under our justice system for anyone charged with a criminal offence to have proper advice and legal counsel, particularly in a case involving a capital charge, and even more so when the accused is illiterate and has no knowledge of his rights. I was naturally a little hot under the collar that there had been no legal counsel present. Although our conversation took place many years ago in my small Peace River office, I clearly remember John Napio. He was a quiet and grave man of ordinary height. He looked me directly in the eyes, before speaking.

"I am John Napio from Calais. I want to tell you something about my son, Louis, who has troubles."

"What kind of trouble?"

"He is in jail in Fort Saskatchewan and will be tried for killing Old Man Ward."

"Yes, I remember the case. But aren't you and he treaty Indians? The Indian Affairs department will appoint a lawyer and will pay for his defence."

"No. They have not. It does not matter. You are to defend him. It's been told."

"Who said so and why?"

"I won't tell you more about this, but Louis can later. Will you help us and see him when he comes here from Fort Saskatchewan?"

"What do you know about the shooting? Did your boy do it?"

"Those at Ghostkeeper's place said Louis shot the old man for no reason—just because he was mad."

"Did Louis tell you about this case? It sounds like a bad one. You know if he is found guilty, he may be hanged?"

"Yes, I have been told this. But I am sure Louis will not die for this."

"Can you tell me the story Louis told you?"

"He doesn't remember. He was drinking too much. All he said was he went to the party and woke up early in the morning in the ditch by Kathleen where Red George Ghostkeeper works on the Northern Alberta Railway section gang. He was sure there was something bad. So he decided not to see his wife but to come to me. I am his father and I have the medicine. He walked at night and hid out in the daytime for two days and came to me next morning."

"Had the police been to your place?"

"Yes. They told me they wanted to talk to Louis about the shooting. I was to let them know if he came home. They would catch him anyway because they had put the RCMP dogs from the south on his trail. When Louis came to my house I told him what would happen. Next morning some RCMP came in a car and took him away."

I agreed to contact the police, the attorney general's department in Edmonton and Indian Affairs officials and see what I could do to help, even though at the time I was already extremely busy. My wife, Beulah, and I had just purchased a large farm and were modernizing the old log house on it. My law practice was active, events were stirring and fermenting for me in the world of politics, but I was intrigued by the Napio case. The man was entitled to the best possible defence even though, in my opinion, he was not a good life insurance policy risk. I believed strongly it was not right for the authorities to deny him counsel. Moreover, after studying a transcript of the inquest proceedings into Ward's death and reading the evidence given at the preliminary inquiry which took place in McLennan, I became genuinely puzzled.

If the evidence sworn to by Indian and Métis witnesses at these proceedings was true, then Louis Napio had deliberately, without provocation, shot and killed a man who was a stranger to him, a man who had done him no harm. It appeared impossible to keep him from the hangman. But something seemed very strange.

Indian Affairs department officials belatedly realized if the case came to trial without adequate preparation for the defence, there would be a real hullabaloo and they would be subjected to severe criticism by the presiding judge. They telephoned, then wrote, asking me to take over the case on the department's behalf. They offered to pay my fees.

I agreed, but only after subjecting them to a severe tongue-lashing for allowing a young native from the bush to appear before an inquiry without advice or legal help, and only on the condition they turn over to me all information in their possession on the Napio case to compensate for the limited time left to prepare for the trial.

Hooray! They sent the entire file, including statements taken by their officials and RCMP investigators within a day or two after the shooting, when it was most likely that witnesses would tell the true story. When the RCMP and Crown lawyers learned later I had the file, they complained strongly to Ottawa. But by then it was too late. I had checked the file and found the widest possible discrepancy between the information it contained and the evidence given at the preliminary hearing and inquest. I was sure witnesses had told department officials the truth and lied or withheld facts later at the hearing and inquest.

Official statements made to officials by witnesses just after the shooting made it plain the party had been a real "moochi-gan", a big drinking affair. In court testimony the majority of witnesses had solemnly sworn there had been no liquor at the Ghostkeepers' that night. They had called it a "tea party," even. No one admitted seeing Napio or anyone else take a drink.

Against the united front of this evidence were statements given by a number of the party guests immediately after the tragedy that there had been drinking during the night; that Louis Napio had been given "many drinks"; that Mary Napio had gone into the bush with a man; and that, according to several witnesses, Louis was "crazy drunk." Two boys, who were outside the cabin that night, said they had seen Napio stagger from the home to a wagon where he picked up his rifle and fired into the air. On hearing the shot most of the guests came running from the cabin. Napio brandished the gun and warned them to stay away, saying he would shoot the first person who moved. Just then Ward came from the shack and moved toward the group and Napio lifted his rifle, fired one shot, killing Ward instantly. He then ran into the bush, throwing his rifle away.

The reason behind the changed stories was clear. The party guests realized some of them would face serious charges for giving liquor to a treaty Indian, especially as it could be a contributing factor to the tragedy. They altered their testimony, and certainly had not been dissuaded from doing so by the police. By banding together in their lies, they thought to make it easier on themselves, at the expense of Louis Napio.

Committing a crime while under the influence of liquor is not a defence to the charge. On the other hand, if it can be established the accused was so drunk he lost control of his senses and could not appreciate the nature and consequences of his act, it might reduce the seriousness of that act. It might make the crime a lesser offence which, in this particular case, could mean reducing the charge from murder to manslaughter.

An early snowfall blanketed the countryside that winter. I wanted to examine the scene of the party and crime so I caught a ride to Mclennan by freight train and hired a sleigh and driver. For the next two days I travelled through the bush visiting the Ghostkeeper cabin, talking to witnesses and examining other threads of circumstances woven into the tapestry of the case. I believe it essential in any issue of this kind to absorb the background and, insofar as is possible, put myself in the position of those present in order to conduct competently the defence and cross-examine the witnesses. Information obtained on this trip confirmed the facts contained in the file I had from Indian Affairs.

After returning to Peace River I had my first interview with Louis Napio. He had been brought to Peace River from Fort Saskatchewan and lodged in the RCMP headquarters cell. I saw him in the basement conference room and during our three-hour interview he confirmed the story in the documents I had. Napio had gone to the party, drunk some beer on the way, and had quite a few more drinks at the cabin. He could not recall how many. He remembered someone saying something about his wife, but from that point on his memory was blank.

Although it has been my experience people charged with a serious crime often rely on selective amnesia, I was certain this was not so in Napio's case. He was a small man who laughed easily and often and, under the circumstances, was extraordinarily cheerful. I asked him if he understood a killing charge was against him and what would happen if convicted.

"Mr. Baldwin, yes. I have been told. But it is all right. The night I got home my father put his hands on my shoulders, looked into my eyes, and told me he had seen ahead. He knew I would not die for this. That night I had the first real sleep in three days. I dreamed the Lord sent me an angel, and the angel told me there would be a trial at Mclennan, and another trial at Peace River, and Mr. Baldwin would defend me, and I would not hang. I know this is true."

The jury trial did take place in Peace River and I used the government file to embarrass and challenge the Crown witnesses. After fumbling and altering their stories, many admitted the truth. At the conclusion of the case for the Crown I was confident things had gone fairly well for us. The prosecution witnesses had been anything but impressive and some of the people at the party had to say Louis Napio was very drunk. This was our case! Yet nothing could alter the fact that Louis Napio had killed Ward. The shooting, though, was something different from the callous, cold-blooded murder portrayed in the pages of the preliminary inquiry report. So the judge had to put our case to the jury.

After a brief discussion with my client, we agreed to call only one witness for the defence, Louis's wife, Mary Napio. She was a personable little woman and I realized her admission of misconduct at the party would have some impact on the jury. Further, she had been in a truck accident since the party and her foot had been amputated. Perhaps this would evoke a measure of sympathy. Once a jury starts moving in your direction, they look for incidents to prop up their views.

The RCMP had been serving as orderlies at the Anglican Athabasca Church hall where the trial was taking place. I arranged with the inspector for two of them to carry the witness in on a stretcher and place her before the jury. The strapping constables who did the honors were not happy about it and their resentment was obvious as they marched from the hall.

I took Mary easily through the preliminaries. She gave her name and told of her marriage, her family, and the party at the Ghostkeepers'. She spoke of the men, including her husband, drinking as they drove the wagon to the cabin. She confirmed there had been much drinking at the party. The guests had consumed beer, whiskey, and moonshine. Louis had been doing his share and more. There had been singing and yelling when they arrived, and it had carried on most of the time. I then asked about her activities.

"Mary, did you go outside the house the night of the party with another man?"

She looked at me and gave a slight nod.

His Lordship interrupted. "Young woman, the reporter cannot take down your head movements. How do you answer the question?"

"Yes, sir, I did."

"And was it with your husband?" I asked.

"No, it was with another man. I went into the bush."

"What happened between you and this man in the bush?"

A long pause and the black eyes in the little round face rolled from the jury to the judge. But there were no words. I tried again, "Mary, this is the first time you have seen your husband since the party. You know he is facing a charge of murder." Again no answer. By now the courtroom was so quiet it would have been possible to hear a pin drop. I walked closer and stood looking down at her. "Mary, it is important, very important that you tell the whole story to the court. Now I want to know what happened, and the jury—those six men sitting over there—want to know what happened after you left the cabin that night."

She gazed straight at me and a grin spread over her chubby face as she answered pointedly, "You know what I did when we went to the bush, Mr. Baldwin."

The court exploded into laughter. Even the judge smiled. Attempting to retrieve the remnants of my dignity I managed a shaky smile as I slunk to my chair.

"Thank you, Mary. That's what I thought. I have no further questions."

The Crown did not see fit to cross-examine but I later heard the jury had placed some stock in her evidence indicating the creation of a circumstance bearing on the subsequent irrational acts of Louis Napio.

After the charge was read, Louis pleaded "not guilty," and elected for trial by jury. He then began skylarking, giggling, and making signs to people he knew in the courtroom. I didn't notice this as I was concentrating on the process of jury selection. Then I saw the judge frown over his glasses at the young man. Turning around, I caught his act and took steps to bring it to an end. I went over to the box where he sat and told him as fiercely as I could, "Look, Louis, it's your neck, not mine. But if I'm going to work for you, then sit still and bloody well behave yourself." He immediately stopped clowning.

At the noon recess the judge passed me on his way out, saying, "I'm glad you stopped your client from acting like an idiot, Ged. From what I've heard so far you've got enough problems without that sort of thing."

Throughout the trial Napio retained his good-natured composure. Actually he appeared so cheerfully unconcerned I was somewhat worried about a possible ill effect of his behavior on the jury. Louis told me he did not know what I was worried about because he had told me already how this case would turn out.

Louis was right. The verdict was manslaughter. The trial judge charged strongly for murder and was manifestly annoyed with the jury for reducing the charge. The jury had snapped up the chance for a lesser verdict founded on the judge's reluctant direction to the jury that a heavily intoxicated man could be unaware of his actions. Napio was sentenced to 15 years in the penitentiary and paroled in five years. He later had an operation to relieve the pressure on his brain. I am told he did not get into any more serious trouble.

This was not the first or last of my associations with a medicine man. During the course of my law practice in the north they appeared more than once, usually as kindly and positive individuals. But not always.

A native couple once brought their 14-year-old daughter to my Peace River office. They claimed she had been raped by the medicine man, who was feared by the other inhabitants of their district. The offence occurred under circumstances which made it likely a conviction could be obtained; however, potential witnesses were too afraid of the man to come forward. I asked if the police had been informed and the father replied they had been, but claimed because the man was an RCMP informer, the police had done nothing. I was satisfied the girl was telling the truth, and determined to see justice done. I had the father swear out a complaint. The police then agreed to serve a summons and also witness subpoenas where needed. I acted as a private prosecutor at the proceedings. The man was convicted and sent to jail. When he was released he found he had lost his hold on the people and was forced to seek a new "practice" in another area.

Another time I was called to High Prairie on behalf of a young native, the son of a woman for whom I had acted on several occasions. The boy was charged with stealing a jeep. Though there was a fifty-fifty chance he might beat this charge, he was certainly guilty of "borrowing" the jeep without permission. We called it "joy-riding" in those days. I found my client lounging in his cell, smoking and reading comics. Like Napio he was remarkably self-composed. I interviewed him and, just as I was leaving, he called out, "Mr. Baldwin, will you get some things for me, some cigarettes and crime comics." I agreed. The constable grinned as I passed him on the way out. "Thank the Lord somebody's helping the guy out. He's been after us since he came in to get him crime comics. It wouldn't look good on the report if the police got crime comics for a prisoner."

The next time I saw my client he was nervous and distraught. I asked what was bugging him. Looking down at the floor he burst out, "It's my brother. I sent him north to get some medicine for me from the man who got Martin Ouelette off for killing his wife. He should have been back by now."

My father had handled the Ouelette case and done a pretty good job of it. I told the boy so.

"Sure," he replied, somewhat defiantly. "But it was really the medicine man who made the difference. That's why I gave my brother all my money to buy some medicine for me."

I went out shaking my head, not having asked if that was why my client had no money for my fees.

Just before the boy was moved to Faust where the trial was to take place, I visited him again. This time he was bubbling with good cheer. His brother had brought the medicine, a small round box containing a few pieces of animal hair and bones and two bird claws.

And truly there were some odd happenings at Faust!

First, the magistrate, who in those days took down his own notes by typewriter during the proceedings, could not get his machine to work. He borrowed a pen to take down the evidence, but that would not work either. I stole a look at my client who was lounging back in his chair with a knowing smirk. The magistrate finally found a working pen and we got on with the trial. Then as the RCMP officer who was prosecuting came to the end of his case, he announced that one witness, essential to the prosecution, had not arrived and would not be available till the end of the month. The magistrate grumbled that it would be a considerable expense for him to return from Peace River for another trial and agreed with me the boy would have to be released on his own bond to await the next trial date.

Deciding to seize the moment I requested a brief adjournment so the magistrate, RCMP, and I could discuss the situation. I suggested a compromise. I would have my client plead guilty to the lesser offence of "joy-riding" if the Crown would agree to a fine and give the accused time to pay it. They agreed, and the boy was fined $25 with three months to pay. In due course the fine was paid and I also received a small fee, probably much less than the medicine man, who no doubt went on to other legal triumphs.

CHAPTER TEN

The Case of the Diving Truck

EARLY ON SEPTEMBER 10, 1954, A RESPECTABLE CITIZEN of the town of Peace River climbed from his bed, went to the front door, and glanced out to see what the day would bring for weather. The house was several hundred yards from the east bank of the river. It had been a night of rain and light fog, but the morning sky was clear, not a cloud in sight. He could easily see the multicolored trees on the distant hills. Then he started. There was a man curled up on the grass next to the sidewalk. He phoned the uptown detachment of the RCMP, then went to see if he could help the man. "What are you doing here? Are you sick or drunk? Who are you? What are you doing on my lawn?"

The stranger, dressed in damp and rumpled clothes, looked around in confusion. "Where am I? How did I get here?" He paused a moment to recollect, then continued. "I was at a party up the Kaufman Hill last night. Then I was with Oslie in his truck. We were driving across the bridge to West Peace River, but what happened next?"

"It must have been some party," the respectable citizen replied drily.

At that moment an RCMP squad car pulled up and a young constable jumped out. The stranger was now showing signs of real pain and distress. Hearing the story, the constable exclaimed: "If you were in the Oslie truck last night, you must be Delorme. Are you okay?"

"Yeah, I'm Delorme, and I feel pretty bad. My back is giving me a lot of misery."

"You come along with me. I'll run you down to the hospital. You were in a bad accident and you're sure lucky to be alive."

Indeed, Delorme was marvelously, incredibly fortunate to count himself among the living that morning. Earlier that same morning, at about 1:00 a.m., Delorme, Delphine Winniandy, and Wilfred Bourassa, a professional cat-skinner with a wooden leg, were passengers in a light delivery truck driven by Oliver Oslie. Travelling west across the Peace River bridge, the truck collided with a Northern Alberta Railway work train, which was backing its way across the bridge.

The train, No. 54, consisted of a locomotive, water tender, and five cars. When its rear car struck the truck, it pushed the truck back some 120 feet, twisting and scraping timbers alongside the track, before it shoved the vehicle over a wooden sidewalk and through the bridge's safety fence. The truck plunged 80 feet to the river below, landing in about four or five feet of water close to the gravel beach. Delphine Winniandy was drowned, Oslie and Bourassa were pulled from the vehicle before the truck went under. But somehow in the confusion Delorme managed to scramble from the cab before rescuers arrived on the scene, make his way to the beach, climb the river bank, and stumble to the lawn of a nearby house before collapsing. How he managed to do this, neither he nor the examining doctor, noting the extent of his injuries, could explain. Moreover, he really did not remember the accident, nor his scramble to safety. Granted, he and his companions had been returning from a party when the accident took place, but there was no compelling evidence he had been drunk. Both Oslie and Bourassa remembered the accident. They recalled the truck turned turtle when it dived into the river.

More importantly, why did the truck and train collide on the bridge at all, a bridge so narrow it was closed to road traffic when a train crossed? A legal battle soon followed.

The operation of the town bridge as a joint rail-and-road vehicle crossing was a carryover from the early days of rail construction. The province had taken over the project when the prime contractor, engaged to build a substantial part of the northern line, suffered a financial collapse. The province finished the planned construction and operated the system, including the line to Waterways and other connections leading to Peace River, Grande Prairie, and Barrhead, until the UFA government of Premier John Brownlee arranged for the sale of the line to a consortium of the CNR and CPR. Many of us in the north would have preferred an exclusive takeover of the line by the CNR; however, Ottawa insisted and the privately owned CPR was allowed in also. As a result, the CNR and CPR general managers alternated, each bringing his own senior people with him. This created a gap between management and the workers who had their roots in the north.

The main line through Mclennan crossed over the Smoky River, then went south of the Peace River. It was called the Edmonton, Dunvegan and British Columbia (ED & BC) line, but more familiarly known as the "Easily Damaged and Badly Constructed" railway. It never got to Dunvegan and only many years later to British Columbia by way of Grande Prairie and Dawson Creek. The line from Mclennan to Peace River crossed the river at that point and then proceeded on the north side to Hines Creek. It was the Central Canada Railway. Both were absorbed into the Northern Alberta Railways system.

The railway bridge at Peace River was the first to span the river. It was constructed at a time when automobiles had limited use in the north. Before the bridge, pedestrians, horse-drawn vehicles, and the few automobiles were ferried across the water. For several weeks each year during the fall freeze and the spring break-up, the ferry did not operate.

The provincial government decided to postpone constructing a second bridge. The existing structure would be used not only for trains, but also for pedestrians, wagons, buggies, and cars. Under normal circumstances no railway company would have tolerated the use of its road bed by anything other than a train. But the province was in the driver's seat and able to call the tune. The CNR-CPR arrangement became a fact under the corporate title of the Northern Alberta Railways. The existing river crossing at Peace River was continued, although some more safety conditions were laid on.

The warning system provided for a vertical swinging gate with a set of flashing red lights and a ringing bell guarding the highway approach on each side of the river. When a train reached a certain section of track an electrical impulse caused the gates to lower and the attached lights and bell were activated. There was also a manual system operated by watchkeepers on duty 24 hours a day. They were stationed in a small cabin slung over the side of the bridge at its approximate centre and with a clear sight of both ends of the bridge. It was the function of the watchkeeper to maintain a constant watch on the bridge. Any approaching train would halt and blow for permission to cross. If the watchkeeper saw no bridge traffic, he would operate a manual switch to lower the gates and then, and only then, give the green light for the train to cross.

In theory, a motorist, finding the highway approach blocked by the gate, could reverse some distance, move onto the exit road, and squeeze past the gate onto the bridge. This would require a remarkable degree of stupidity as well as a high level of driving skill. Both approaches were narrow and backing past the barrier of poles separating the entry and exit roads would not be easy. The width of the roadway was just 15 feet with the two steel rails running down the centre. Given the width of the locomotive and even greater dimensions of the freight cars, it was simply not possible for a car and train to pass on the bridge. Everyone living in the area knew that.

Work train No. 54 was called by the dispatcher at the Northern Alberta Railway's divisional point of Mclennan, some 60 miles southeast of Peace River, at 9:00 p.m. September 9. Its ultimate destination was Roma, located at the top of the valley just west of Peace River, and the first siding out of "the hole," as the valley was called. Leaving Mclennan at about 9:45 p.m., it was made-up of the engine, tender, five loaded cars, and five empties, including a water car to be filled at the tank immediately west of the bridge, then taken to Roma along with supplies for the B&B gang (the bridge building crew working out of Roma). The work train had a crew of five, an engineer, conductor, fireman, and two trainmen.

No. 54 rattled down the long hill east of town after midnight and was then split on the level grade near the station on the east side of the bridge. The engine, tender, and five cars, including the empty water car at the rear, moved across the bridge. After taking on water first, the engine pulled past the tank so the water car could be filled. It then began to reverse across the bridge with the water car in the lead. At about the same time, Oliver Oslie was steering his light delivery truck onto the eastern end of the bridge.

Oslie was a cook who hired on with various construction and

oil exploration outfits and lived between jobs in his small cabin below the bridge on the north side of town. After supper on the evening of September 9, he cleaned up and drove to town where he met with friends. Oslie had a few beers with them in the hotel and, just before the 10:00 p.m. closing, he bumped into a woman acquaintance who invited him to a party at her house. Oslie drove her to her house, located on a bumpy, twisting trail just off the main road leading up Kaufman Hill, northeast of town.

The party was in progress when they arrived, and Oslie took in a small case of beer he had purchased. He stayed less than three hours and had one or two more beers. There was no indication he was drunk, nor noticeably under the influence. Actually, Oslie was not a heavy drinker. Between jobs he sometimes visited a bar, mainly to meet and talk with friends. Just as he was leaving, Wilfred Bourassa, the one-legged cat-skinner, who lived near Oslie, came clumping up to ask for a ride home. "Sure," Oslie replied. "I'm going straight home."

The two were about to climb into the truck when Delorme hailed Oslie and requested a lift to his place for himself and his girlfriend, Delphine Winniandy. Delorme lived on the west side of the river, and the good-natured Oslie agreed, even though it would mean a trip across the bridge. However, mindful of his promise to Bourassa, he said he would drop the cat-skinner off first.

Oslie was driving slowly down the difficult, winding trail into town, then onto the main street leading to the district under the bridge where he and Bourassa lived, when he was confronted by a large road excavation. It was guarded by a construction barrier with flashing lights. This was enough to block his approach to Bourassa's home by that route. He decided then to take Delorme and Winniandy home first. With some difficulty he backed away from the road obstruction and turned around, then drove by a different street to the eastern approach to the bridge.

The bridge is about 1,800 feet long and bearing in mind that the truck and train collided just east of the middle section, each must have begun crossing the bridge about the same time because it proved difficult to determine which was first, in spite of the evidence given by a number of witnesses at later proceedings. Both probably travelled at similar speeds.

The railway held its own inquiry. There was also an inquest into the death of Winniandy and a review of the facts in connection with a proposed criminal proceeding. Oslie and Bourassa, too, launched an action against the company. They were examined for discovery. There were similar examinations of certain officers and agents of the Northern Alberta Railways. The trial itself was held before a judge without a jury. Finally, there was an appeal to the appellate division of the supreme court taken by the railway company from the trial judgment awarding damages to Oslie and Bourassa.

The physical evidence was not disputed. It made crystal clear that the rear end of the water car caught the truck just east of the centre of the bridge, shoved it back, then hoisted it over the side to the river below. Shortly after an emergency call was placed to the police from the railway station, RCMP Corporal Bill Brace and a constable were on the scene with rope, lights, and other equipment, and rescue operations were carried out speedily and efficiently enough to save Oslie and Bourassa.

The police found the truck on its side, its rear wheels close to the shore, and its cab in about five feet of water. The woman, Delphine Winniandy, was totally submerged. She was pulled out and an unsuccessful attempt made to revive her. Oslie was behind the wheel with the water just reaching his mouth. Bourassa, who was taller and sitting in a more upright position, was on the other side of the cab with the water just below his chin. While the policemen held the two men above water, several of the train crew pulled them from the truck. It was a difficult and ticklish operation as the truck had to be lifted somewhat to get Oslie from behind the wheel and out the door.

When Bourassa was being lifted from the beach onto a stretcher, he asked the police to be careful of his leg, referring to his sound leg which had been injured. His rescuers, not aware he had a wooden leg, noted it was twisted. They carefully placed him on a stretcher and only when they reached the hospital did they learn how carefully they had protected his wooden leg. This caused some amusement at the trial.

There was no sign of any other passenger in the truck and it was not until some hours later, when Oslie was able to talk, that the authorities learned that another man called Delorme had been in the truck.

I talked to Delorme on several occasions, both in the hospital and after he was released. I wanted to know if he could give me some firm information on his escape from the truck and how he had made his way up the river bank to the house where he was found. But he could only shake his head and say that he had no recollection. As I studied the case, talked to doctors, and did a little reading on the subject, I became convinced that the nightmare of the accident—meeting the train head on, plunging from the bridge with the truck turning in mid-air, landing in the river, then the water rising in the cab—had produced shock and a limited amnesia in Delorme.

Oslie was hospitalized for 47 days; Bourassa was not released from hospital for two months. Each had fractured ribs and vertebrae. Oslie also had a fractured vertebra, a fractured pelvis, plus some minor injuries. Bourassa's right leg was broken and his lung collapsed. Delorme had several broken ribs and a badly twisted back. Yet all three were alive and in the course of time each went about his usual way of life.

Earlier I referred to miracles! What a catalogue of luck marked these three. Not being crushed by the train. Falling at the right place—twenty feet further to the west and they'd have all been drowned in water well over the height of the truck. They'd have been swept downstream by the current and the truck would have gone under. Twenty feet more to the east and they'd have landed on hard, harsh, rough gravel and most likely would have suffered fatal injuries. Then there was the remarkable efficiency shown by the police patrol in reaching the scene of the accident, and their prompt and effective teamwork in pulling the two men out, which certainly saved at least Oslie's life.

The crucial question remained: who was really at fault.

The top officials and managerial staff, seconded from either the CNR or the CPR, brought to the northern rail operations much of the semi-divine, autocratic presumption they had acquired with the two main lines. Their presumption was even more noticeable because of the less-than-subtle means they used. When an unusual accident like Oslie's occurred, the railway's immediate, automatic reaction was to insist that, naturally, they had done all they were required to do, everything according to the general running regulations as well as the special rules for the bridge. Anything else was unthinkable. That being so and unchallengable then, they felt, Oslie simply had to be in the wrong. He must have been mad or drunk, deliberately going onto the bridge by the exit road in defiance of all warnings and common sense, and by this imprudence, putting the truck and its occupants at risk. This attitude of the railway was consistent throughout the long series of legal battles which unfolded out of this extraordinary accident.

Oslie's response, supported by Bourassa, was that they were not damn fools, they had lived in Peace River for many years, crossed the bridge often, knew the warning system, and would not have ventured onto the bridge at 1:00 a.m. had there been a closed gate, red flashing lights, bells ringing. The train came onto the bridge without any warning.

The railway company had representation at the inquest and a watching brief. They proceeded in a sustained and stubborn attempt—sometimes working with the authorities—checking, researching, and digging into all the facts. This was their right, but it also showed plainly their contention that Oslie deliberately ignored the signals because he was drunk or badly impaired. If they could convince a court of this, it would go a long way toward freeing them from responsibility for the death and injuries and property damage.

The widest and most detailed inquiries were made to find witnesses from the bars and the Testawich party who could testify to this. None came forward.

In fact, neither the police nor the railway were able to make a court case that Oslie's condition rendered him incapable of properly driving his truck that night. Oslie admitted only to drinking a few beers between 8:30 p.m. and midnight on September 9, 1954. On the other hand, the first time I heard the railway crew accounts, they sounded too good to be true. Reading and re-reading earlier evidence in preparation for the trial showed that each rule, each regulation, each and every safety precaution had been scrupulously followed. And, of course, several witnesses were available to testify to each such action.

Experienced trial lawyers are cynical and suspicious of large masses of evidence that dovetail beautifully like parts of a jigsaw puzzle. I was first brought into the picture when my firm was retained to act for Oslie in respect of proposed criminal proceedings, based on the allegation of negligent driving leading to the death of Delphine Winniandy. It was not a very robust case. I had the feeling the local RCMP were not pushing it too hard. I guessed instructions probably came from Edmonton and that railway officials were using their muscle to persuade the police to make these charges. If the Northern Alberta Railway really were attempting to influence the police, then their actions backfired. As witnesses were subjected to vigorous cross-examination, the artificial quality of the company's nicely designed case became apparent. The case suddenly started to come apart. Oslie was in the clear.

Having been put to the cost as well as the harassment of making a defence, Oslie was annoyed and upset by the chivvying and persecution. He discussed bringing an action against the Northern Alberta Railway based on its negligence in operating the train and its failure to observe safety regulations. Normally, Oslie was a most easy-going sort of fellow and I am convinced that if he had been left alone, he would have been willing to forget the entire business. We agreed to go ahead with the case on behalf of him and Bourassa. Delorme had left the area, and there appeared no person in sight to represent the dead woman's estate.

The civil action would not be a jury trial. Even so, a bias lay in the public mind against railway companies, particularly in the Peace River area. Our Northern Alberta Railway was a subservient feeder for the other two railways, and the people of Peace River lost out on the deal. This bias did not in general apply to most of the rail workers. They fitted into the community life of the small northern towns. It was directed against the company and its management officials who were often suspect in the minds of the average person. In a trial of this kind, community attitude was folded into the proceedings and became a factor that could not be ignored.

The civil action for damages came on before Mr. Justice Neil Primrose at Peace River on October 17, 1956, more than two years after the accident. Apart from evidence by doctors as to the extent of personal injuries and the number of work months lost, the case for Oslie and Bourassa consisted of their own testimony, portions of the examinations for discovery of certain railway officials, and certain cross-examination answers from defence witnesses. There was also the testimony of several people called to lay before the court physical evidence. Corporal Brace, the first person to arrive at the scene of the accident, testified in part:

> ... arrived at approximately five minutes after it happened, at 1:30 in the morning. Noticed a vehicle several feet out from shore in the river toppled over on its (driver's) side in about four feet of water. Constable Nagy and I dived into the water and with the aid of our flashlights noted three passengers in the vehicle. One was completely submerged in water up to his chin and he was identified as Mr. Bourassa. Another man was submerged in water possibly up to his mouth, later identified as Mr. Oslie. The third was completely submerged. We groped around, and located Delphine Winniandy, and brought her above the surface, and holding her with one hand, we were able to grab Mr. Oslie's hair and hold him above the surface to prevent drowning, Constable Nagy held Mr. Bourassa's head above the water to prevent him from drowning. Somehow, between the two of us, and still holding the other two parties, we were able to get Mr. Bourassa out of the top of the truck by opening the door and lifting him up and placing him on top of the truck. Then we were able to release Delphine Winniandy and take her to shore. I commenced artificial respiration. Constable Nagy was still holding Mr. Oslie above the surface. When help arrived we were able to lift the truck sufficiently to take out Mr. Oslie, who was pinned behind the steering wheel of the truck, and take him to the bank. They were treated for shock and arrangements made for their ambulance.

The stiff language of this official report belies the outstanding actions of Brace and Nagy. Under cross-examination, Brace said there was an odor of beer in the truck's cab.

Oslie and Bourassa were not good witnesses. At times they were hesitant; at best, steady and plodding. Nonetheless, their evidence, coming after the account of the spectacular action of the river rescue, had a dramatic quality. They told of turning back from the road construction in town and heading for the bridge. It was a dark night with a very slight mist. There was no sign of any light on the bridge. It was pitch black. The barrier was raised. Yes, Oslie knew the bridge well and under no consideration would he venture onto the crossing against a gate, lights, and the bell. Oslie and Bourassa spoke quietly of moving at a low speed on the bridge, then catching sight of the rear end of the train's back car as it came inexorably toward them, the nightmare of that. At the time they thought they were still on the eastern half of the bridge.

Oslie stopped the truck and put it into reverse; all the while the train relentlessly moved toward them. Although the train was gaining on them, Oslie at first managed to go backwards for some distance. Then one of the truck's rear wheels came up against the foot-high curb between the roadbed and sidewalk. They were brought to a standstill. Oslie tried to straighten the truck. One of them, probably Bourassa, shouted, "Should we bail out?" By then it was too late.

The back end of the water car collided with the truck and started to shove them back. At first the truck managed to stay upright, although it was banged and scraped against first one curb then the other, until it twisted too far sideways and was pushed over the curb, across the sidewalk, through the wooden railing, overturning in the air, and landing on its side in the river below.

Neither Oslie or Bourassa were seriously hurt by the savage mauling they received in cross-examination. In fact, as is sometimes the case, they rallied and firmed up certain parts of their respective narratives, which had been weak under their original questioning. Their stories were believable because they came from the same stuff as ordinary people and used the same language ordinary people knew and understood; there was a quality of simplicity in their stories. The judge could be seen observing them very closely. He then settled back as if he accepted their bona fides. Certainly, he made no strenuous attempt to question them himself or challenge in any way.

When we closed the case for the plaintiff, there was little doubt we had more than discharged the onus which rests on any plaintiff in a civil action. It would now be necessary for the Northern Alberta Railway and its battery of lawyers to produce a powerful defence. Anxiety about the position of the company, fear for their jobs, and fear of the loss of demerit points inspired the train crew to put their best foot forward in the stories they gave from the box.

The bridge tender and each of the train's crew were witnesses as were several experts knowledgeable about the warning system and the equipment operated by the on-duty watchman in the cabin. Other technical evidence was tendered about the bridge—its length and width—as well as the stopping time of the train, and other such background information. In order to demolish the prima facie case established by the plaintiffs, the company had to show Oslie and Bourassa were lying, and make it very clear those operating the train and signal system had complied fully with the regulations. In attempting this, they forced the pace too much. There was an artificial gloss, a lack of spontaneity, an overall impression of a virtuoso effort. It just did not wash. The witnesses made several odd statements.

For example, the railway reconstruction of the events of that morning produced three witnesses who could all assert they had seen the green light to proceed because they were all inside the locomotive looking out the left as the train backed up with the track curving left. Usually in such a situation the engineer sits on the right-hand side of the cab and the fireman on the left to relay to the engineer any signals or messages he observes. But that night there was also a trainman on the left looking anxiously ahead for signals. In addition, at this quiet place at 1:30 a.m., the engineer himself inexplicably considered it essential that he, too, should leave his controls and move over to the left side. Three witnesses now claimed, "Yes, we saw the green light to proceed given by the bridge tender; yes, we saw the road barrier lights come down and start flashing before the train entered the bridge."

Similarly, according to his evidence, the bridge tender had done all he was required to do. But on this particular night, the bridge tender thought it would be a good idea to leave his warm, comfortable cabin, come out to the side of the bridge, and wave to the men working the train on a raw, dark, misty night. As he asserted, "I saw the trainman at the point with his signal lantern. I saw the others, too. At the time there was no sign of the truck or its lights."

The most bizarre statement came from the trainman, who claimed he was riding the point at the rear of the water car. He contended he saw the truck lights appear on the bridge, started to signal to the engineer and, when he saw there was going to be a crash, jumped off. He testified, "I ran *west* from the point of impact to the locomotive and came to it just as it stopped." If this were true, it would have put the engine, at least, west of the point of impact, more than 120 feet west of the hole in the bridge where the truck was pushed over. All the other witnesses claimed the engine came to a halt just a few feet *east* of this hole.

The crew was locked into their set of responses because that was what they had reported to the company just after the accident. It was an extraordinary exhibition.

On the major points at issue, the four members of the train crew all contended that after the water car was filled, the engineer blew a signal for the bridge tender to warn him they were ready to back across the bridge. At that time one trainman was at the point and the other three in the engine cab. They all saw the green light given by the bridge tender. There were no car lights on the bridge, and they all watched the red flashing lights as the gate swung into place on the west approach. The bridge tender told the same story, but added that after he had stepped out of this warm cabin to "watch the train go by," he saw the lights of a motor vehicle flicker at the east approach to the bridge.

The trial was concluded late in the evening. The judge, who was travelling back the next day, announced he would reserve his decision. It would be sent to counsel in a few days. I had the impression the judge had made up his mind, but wanted to check through his notes, then dictate written reasons for his judgment. A decision against the railway company could mean an appeal. Any finding had to be clearly related to the evidence on record. The judgment was dictated October 23, 1956 and we received it a few days later. Judgment was for the plaintiffs.

On the major issues as to the facts which had divided the parties, the judge made the following findings:

"Although he had been drinking, I am unable to find that Oslie was intoxicated, or his driving was affected, and he gave reasonable explanation of the manner in which he drove on the bridge, which I accept.

"I can only find that the arm (gate) was up as he entered.

"I find they (the crew) were negligent in not seeing the truck sooner, and signalling for an emergency stop.

"In my view he (the engineer) was negligent in travelling

too fast, in failing to see the truck, and in failing to stop before striking the plaintiff's truck.

"I find he (the trainman at the point) was negligent in failing to see the truck sooner and signal for an emergency stop."

These and other findings seemed to be a most formidable obstacle to an appeal, but the company bulled ahead anyway. The appeal was heard in March 1957 before Chief Justice Ford and three other judges, but it was dismissed. The company took its lumps and the diving truck became an item in law and rail statistics.

I do not mean to suggest there was a carefully contrived plot between the company and these employees to concoct a story which would do in Oslie and Bourassa. Company executives and workmen did not share that close a relationship. But there was a close feeling of camaraderie between workers, particularly in the north. It involved more than belonging to the same union. They acted to protect one another. For example, not many years after the bridge case, a train crew error just missed becoming a tragedy. It occurred at Judah, the first siding at the top of the east hill out of Peace River. The siding overlooks the Peace and Smoky River junction at the top of a very steep grade. The track has a number of curves overlooking spots where rock slides have taken place along the east side of the track. A freight train was shunting cars there. Instead of being braked, a freight car at the end of the train had been given a shove. It rolled slowly to the top of the grade and then, to the horror of the crew, started to move down on its own. Miraculously the car clung to the tracks. For several miles of descent it was travelling at a breakneck speed.

It reached level grade at the bottom of the hill and flashed past the amazed man on duty at the station, sped across the bridge, and continued some distance up the west hill before the force of gravity intervened and it started down again, re-crossed the bridge and was still moving smartly when it reached the station a second time. Someone managed to jump aboard the car and brake it to a stop. A few minutes later the frightened crew of the freight train came trundling down with their engine and the errant car was taken into custody.

By the grace of heaven, it was too early in the morning for

there to have been any automobile traffic on the bridge. The incident was never reported. It might never have come to the knowledge of company authorities if the Northern Alberta Railway manager, visiting Peace River, had not been asked by an innocent lady, "Wasn't it really lucky that no car was on the bridge when that freight car came whizzing over?"

There may also be those who feel I make too much of a latent hostility to the rail companies. This attitude was a carryover from earlier days in western Canada and the western United States. I had several other trials against these companies, and there was always some element of this feeling.

John Diefenbaker, in one of his reminiscing moods in the lobby of the House of Commons, told a story about a farmer from the western Canadian prairies. One morning he discovered two of his purebred cattle dead. Later in the day he was told the price of wheat had fallen. Then he received a telephone call from his son who had failed his college exams. Glowering and feeling very low, the farmer walked out to his best field of wheat, ripening beautifully and looking to be good for at least 40 bushels to the acre. As he reached the far edge of the field of wheat, he could see an ominous thunder cloud bearing in his direction. Sure enough, before he reached home, down came the heavy rain, then a devastating burst of hail, beating much of his crop to the ground. Losing all control, the farmer shook his fist at the sky and yelled, "Now damn the CPR!"

CHAPTER ELEVEN

Rails North

THE ENORMOUS STRETCH OF CANADA FROM THE AT-
lantic to the Pacific and the thin population it sustains underline
the importance of transportation, particularly rail, in the building of this country. The east-west aspect of our life as a nation,
running against the current of geography and economics, has
been dealt with so often and so eloquently that it is interwoven
into the fabric of our history. The move to the north, to our third
ocean, came later, waiting for the most part upon the airplane,
although there were several northern rail lines built in years
past. One caused quite a controversy.

The fight revolved around building 440 miles of rail line to the
lead-zinc mine at Pine Point, with a branch to Hay River on the
south shore of Great Slave Lake. Consolidated Mining and
Smelting was developing the mine. Ore had been discovered
there many years ago by people travelling to the Yukon in search
of gold. Over the years several unsuccessful attempts had been
made to mine it and title ultimately passed to the Consolidated
people. They decided it was worthwhile proceeding at Pine
Point when it became difficult and expensive to process ore at
their major plant in Trail. Much of the Pine Point ore was close to
the surface and could be easily mined. However, a rail link to
carry out the Pine Point ore to Trail for refining would be essential. There were two possible routes—an east route and a west
route.

The east route proposed would run the line north from Fort
McMurray along the west bank of the Athabasca River, curve
west around Lake Athabasca and Lake Clair—the large swampy
water west of Lake Athabasca—then cross over the Peace River

near Peace Point, and east toward the Slave River, then to Pine Point through Wood Buffalo Park, and on into Hay River.

The west route proposed would be built north from Peace River through the rich farming districts lying north of Grimshaw, through Manning, Paddle Prairie, Keg River, High Level, Fort Vermilion, then directly to Hay River with a branch line to Pine Point.

If people counted for something, the west route was the only one to choose. Thousands of men and women had sweated and toiled to develop these farming districts and their communities. Many came north in the belief and the promise that a northern railway would eventually be built to service their needs. On the other hand, money, big money, corporate power, strong federal government influence, all heavily weighted the scales for the east route. The combination of bureaucracy and some of the big names in mining, finance, and transportation presented a formidable, impressive challenge. It would not easily be beaten.

I was interested in the controversy. Partly on that account I agreed in 1956 to accept the nomination as candidate for the Progressive Conservative party. The federal election was expected in 1957. At the time there was little competition for the job. The Progressive Conservatives had never polled more than a small percentage of votes in earlier elections. To talk seriously of sending a member to Ottawa took some courage, or stupidity. The prospect of my being elected Member of Parliament was not a glittering one. At my nomination convention there were less than twenty people present, about a third of whom were relatives. Shortly after my nomination, however, things started to change and my fortunes looked a lot better. Party leader George Drew resigned. Then in 1956 in Ottawa, the first big Canadian political convention with all the color, hoopla, and excitement of an American convention was held. John Diefenbaker was elected Progressive Conservative leader with a big majority. Interest in our party increased. We began to look more like a national group than an east-based minority. We were engaging the attention of the media, pulling support to the party, and establishing a great base for the forthcoming campaign.

One of the new matters raised as part of our election platform was the question of northern development. It was dubbed the "Roads to Resources" program, later ridiculed by both Mike

Pearson and the Co-operative Commonwealth Federation, the old CCF, as the "Igloo-to-Igloo" policy. Nonetheless, the Canadian people warmed to the idea of building highways from mid-Canada into the north. It fitted, of course, right into the rail issue with which I was concerned. When the policy was being debated at the convention, I had a chance to move an amendment to include rail construction as part of the deal. In spite of some discouragement from those in charge, the amendment was approved. Then, when Diefenbaker came north to speak on my behalf, he endorsed the rail proposal. Subsequently, the building of the northern railway and the route it would follow became a potent election issue in the northwestern part of Canada, particularly so in Peace River.

The provinces were divided as to which route was better. Saskatchewan, naturally, was for an east route. British Columbia came out strongly for a west route. In the beginning Alberta leaned to the east, but later changed. The Manning Social Credit government strongly endorsed construction through the Peace River area. As a result, there were inquiries—both federal and provincial—royal commissions, petitions, and letters to newspapers, speeches in Parliament, briefs filed. Premier W.A.C. Bennet of British Columbia sent us a very bright and urbane young lawyer called Arthur Fouks and an equally brilliant transportation and freight expert, Jack Guest, to work with our group lobbying for the west route.

While the battle raged on, a federal election had taken place. John Diefenbaker was Prime Mininster with a minority Parliament. He began to steam right ahead with the "Roads to Resources" program, but the Progressive Conservative government hesitated over the final decision on the northern railway.

I, too, had been elected in 1958. Having directed much of my own campaign to the railway issue, I arrived in Ottawa, confidently expecting doors to swing open, civil servants to flood me with information, and ministers to seek my advice on the issue of new rail construction and any other great national project.

How very naive I was.

Northern rail construction, in particular, was a vexed question. I was met with closed doors.

The situation deteriorated still further, we thought, when Alvin Hamilton of Saskatchewan was appointed Minister of Indian and Northern Affairs. He threw his weight toward building the railway along the east route as expected. At one time it had appeared a decision to build the railway along the east route was imminent. In 1958 it was obvious that because the government had obtained the largest majority ever, there was no reason for them to be concerned with public thinking, with the numbers of voters affected by a decision.

I recall attending a special caucus in a Commons committee room with members from Alberta and British Columbia. Several cabinet ministers were there. The Minister of Indian and Northern Affairs had a stand set up with some charts. He proceeded to state the official position, one based on wrong statistics, wrong arguments—wrong socially, economically, and factually. I was allowed a few minutes to reply, but the division bells rang for a vote in the House before I had finished my remarks. The meeting ended, without endorsing the government position. I thought it a reasonably satisfactory outcome. It left the matter open.

It had always been my feeling that the Prime Minister was not clearly in favor of the east route, which was the official stand. I had already sent word I would feel free to follow an independent position if I had to; others were also on our side. Fortunately, however, this was never necessary.

Diefenbaker was persuaded to establish an inquiry—the Great Slave Lake Railway Royal Commission. He chose three members for the commission. One was John Anderson-Thomson. The others were Mr. Justice Marshall E. Manning and Professor W.D. Gainer of the University of Alberta. I acted as unpaid counsel for a citizen lobby group of Peace River area Chambers of Commerce and other organizations united to advocate the construction of a route through our area.

In any major rail construction work of this kind it becomes necessary to identify and set out the various strategic cost factors. Therefore, it is important to have access to the data upon which they are being developed; in this case, the nature of the terrain to be traversed by the right-of-way; the overall grade of the terrain; what would be the access to construction material along the route; the proximity of parallel transportation facilities for supplying construction crews; the potential freight to be carried, and so forth. Other people involved in the debate seemed to have access to this sort of information. Yet right from the start we could not get hold of data in the records of government departments, in the files of the rail companies or those of the mining corporations. In particular, we seemed to be stymied in our requests to the Department of Indian and Northern Affairs. Later it became obvious to us why we were having so many problems securing information. Much of the data we wanted would build a convincing case for the west route, not the supposedly better east route.

The Department of Indian and Northern Affairs particularly seemed determined that the railway must follow the east route. As a result, I believe, all of the corporations involved—the CNR, the CPR, Consolidated Mining, Pine Point Mines—had simply fallen into line with what they perceived to be official government thinking. They wanted construction to start, sooner not later, and they realized the government would be guaranteeing the costs of construction and regulating freight rates. If the department wanted to arrange matters so the railway went from Fort McMurray to Pine Point and Hay River, it was all right with them. Later, I learned even the engineering staff of the CNR had felt the west route the more sensible way.

This was a pattern I was to see repeated time after time in my years in the House of Commons. Important decisions would be made in the dark closets of government departments and agencies because there were officials willing to tailor situations to fit the narrow pattern of bureaucratic desire. The decision might have little to do with the public's will or need in such matters. More often than not, the public were not privy to the making of the judgments which would affect them, neither they nor the private Members of Parliament who represented them. The size of our national debt and the yearly budget deficit, I feel, bear an eloquent testimony to the kinds of decisions made in dark closets that result in improperly planned and executed programs.

After the government appointed the royal commission, things looked brighter. Of the three members—Anderson-Thomson, Manning, and Gainer—Anderson-Thomson proved to be a real asset in our argument. Anderson-Thomson was a wiry, pipe-smoking, tough-minded character from Yellowknife. He was one of the early settlers in that community, knew the people of the north well, and had extensive professional experience in the north as a surveyor and an engineer. He used all of this background skilfully, and at times rudely, to puncture the mishmash of inaccuracies brought forward by the federal government and the railway and mining companies during the commission's hearings.

In the main, sittings were held in Peace River, Fort McMurray, Yellowknife, and Edmonton. Sitting across from us were officials of the government and the companies with their senior counsel and professional experts hovering about. They produced a variety of witnesses and material for their side. I recall listening to one itinerant prospector solemnly assure the commissioners he was sure of a large mineral deposit along the east route. Asked for proof, he explained that in travelling through the district he had observed several heavy summer electrical storms. Each time lightning seemed to hit one particular spot. He explained he knew this would not be happening if the electricity were not attracted by some mineral body. He admitted that so far in his searching he just had not yet located it. There was a loud snort of derision from Anderson-Thomson.

The CNR presented an extensive brief and called witnesses to support their position. They had a platoon of top officials—lawyers, engineers, economists. Their chief counsel produced their star witness with an especial flourish. He was a young economist, overloaded with degrees and academic honors. The chief counsel said his witness was the one person the company thought most competent to deal with the issues presented by the two proposed rail lines, the east route and the west route.

It was important to establish what additional freight would be carried by the rail line, wherever it ran. There would be lead-zinc concentrates from Pine Point to be taken south. General supplies could be brought in. The agricultural produce from the north area of Peace River was a possible freight, but the railway companies thought it would be a money-losing proposition and should be rejected, therefore. (Never mind that farmers there were paying a haulage charge of $.50 to $.75 a bushel just to bring their grain over roads too often impassable to the present railhead.) Lumber was another key product. It might be a freight to consider.

The CNR's star witness seemed to be assured that we all understood the importance of these key factors. Then he used his pointer to indicate on his map an area on the Peace River side of the region. He cooly informed the commissioners that the existing Northern Alberta Railway sytem was close enough to carry any production from logging in that area. New rail construction along a proposed west route was unnecessary. He then placed his pointer on another section of the map. Here, he breathlessly informed us, was one of the great untouched forests of the north. It would produce a huge quantity of lumber on a permanent yield basis. This would make the east route not just desirable, but a necessity. The Pine Point rail addition could be very much a paying proposition. As he spoke, he pointed to the Wood Buffalo National Park. Never did one person so definitively and dramatically destroy his own credibility and the case of the company he represented.

There was much good timber lying out along the west route but it was far north of the existing rail line and would require a railroad in order to develop. Most certainly it was not where the witness had indicated. On the other hand, the timber indicated on the east route lay within the great Wood Buffalo National Park. Those lands under the terms of the National Parks Act cannot be logged extensively. Most damning of all, however, were the statistics he quoted of projected annual yield of timber from the park. The figures seemed incredibly, unbelievably high. We demanded proof.

With a dramatic gesture, counsel for the CNR produced a letter from the Department of Indian and Northern Affairs documenting the figures. We checked. Through sheer incompetence, or perhaps even deliberately, the department had confused board feet with cubic!

The star witness was shocked; the CNR looked stupid; the department officials were thoroughly flustered.

After some months of hearings, the commission went into retirement to consider the evidence and write the report. This took some time. What eventually emerged was a divided report. Anderson-Thomson was solidly for the west route; Gainer was equally strong for the east; Manning generally favored the west route, but less enthusiastically than Anderson-Thomson. We were almost back to square one again.

In due course, Diefenbaker supported the people against the

corporations and the government departments. The line was started on the west route. It was completed in 1964 at an official ceremony close to the Northwest Territories border. I still have two ceremonial spikes given to those who were in it at the finish. The rail line, I am pleased to add, was one of the rare government projects built at less than the original estimated cost, well within the funds appropriated by Parliament, and within the time allocated. Just as important, it paid for its costs within a comparatively short period.

If there is an epilogue to this tale, it may be the reception Beulah and I attended to commemorate the building of the railway. Among the very convivial guests were many of my opponents from that debate—the rail companies, the mining corporations, and the government departments. There was a film and there were speeches. I was flabbergasted to hear one of the CNR engineers say this line was built the only way it could be built, by the only possible route, the west route, and it had to go this way or it might never have been constructed at all.

Years later I found a partial explanation for the stubborn insistence of the Department of Indian and Northern Affairs upon the east route. The Township of Fort Smith, then the capital of the Northwest Territories, and a habitation generously supplied with federal civil servants, was located not far from the proposed east route. At that time there was no access to Fort Smith by highway. Federal officials, their families, and their possessions were compelled to come north by aircraft or by boat in the summer. Prior to the time of the dispute over the west and the east routes, a plan had been drawn showing a rail line to Fort Smith. That may have been the real benefit of the east route all along from the point of view of the Department of Indian and Northern Affairs—to make life more convenient for the federal civil servants of Fort Smith.

CHAPTER TWELVE

Rapeseed Renewed

DURING THE SECOND WORLD WAR, THE ALLIED COUN-tries experienced a serious shortage of an essential marine lubricant. It had been obtained before the war from countries that were now in enemy hands. What to do? Experiments showed that rapeseed could produce an acceptable substitute. Meetings were held among the Allies to figure out how to cope with the crisis. It was learned that Canada had some experience, albeit limited, in growing rapeseed, as well as having the right soil and weather conditions. The decision was made to turn the task over to us, although the rapeseed that had been grown in Canada was a somewhat different variety than what was wanted now. It had been a seed brought over from Europe that had never really caught on with our farmers. There had never been a lot grown.

The task of finding enough rapeseed to meet the need of the Allies for a marine lubricant was put in the lap of the Canadian Wheat Board. Board officials and government people moved quickly. The board fixed a price and selected a strain of seed everyone hoped would be suitable. Because a northern climate was required, the board turned to northern Saskatchewan and the Peace River area. A great many farmers heeded the call. Before long an abundance of suitable grain was available for market and the shortage overcome. The farmers of the north had met the challenge. In doing so, they had become very knowl-edgeable about a rather novel agricultural product. Then came the end of the war. As is so often the case, the federal govern-ment forgot everything accomplished by those who had respon-ded to the call for help. The Canadian Wheat Board abolished its guaranteed price for rapeseed; the railways established higher freight rates; and the net amount payable to growers was dramatically decreased.

Many farmers just shrugged it off as one more illustration of government stupidity, and got out of growing rapeseed as fast as they could. But others refused to allow the crop to be written off without putting up a good fight for it.

Those who till the soil are by inclination and actual life experience the world's greatest individualists. They are much more likely to look to their own efforts for reward than to the rest of society. Nor is it merely the reward of money. To plow and seed, cultivate and harvest, to see fields covered with the pastel yellow of the rapeseed plant for many was an achievement by itself. They did not want to surrender the accomplishment as worthless.

I first heard of the difficulties faced by those growing rapeseed when some clients who were in my law office on other business told me about it. I wrote some officials in the provincial government, but without any result. Later on, about 1955 or 1956, some of the same farmers returned as part of a delegation. Said their spokesman, "Mr. Baldwin, when the government asked us to produce rapeseed rather than wheat, we did. We learned the best methods to adapt it to our soil. We are pretty good at growing rapeseed. We have been in touch with others and with our farm organizations so we believe there is a market in Europe and in Asia for our crop. We feel very strongly, in fact, that the government should be using its considerable resources to strengthen our production of rapeseed, but they are not. They are letting us down badly."

I agreed to help. The next time I was in Edmonton I did some checking. The farm belt in northern Saskatchewan and the Peace River area had indeed developed this new crop to a stage where it was a viable alternative to other grains. Many thousands of farmers could be concerned with the future of rapeseed. I then got in touch with a former Member of Parliament from Moose Jaw, Saskatchewan, by the name of John Gordon Ross. He, too, was doing his best to organize protests to put some pressure on Ottawa.

During the forthcoming 1957 and 1958 federal election campaigns, I dealt with the issue. When Parliament met after my election in 1958, I found another ally in the person of Reynold Rapp, the very hard-working and conscientious Member of Parliament from the constituency of Humboldt-Melfort-Tisdale in northern Saskatchewan. Together, we asked a number of questions in the House, raised the problem at committee meetings, and harassed ministers whose departments ought to be involved. At first we had precious little satisfaction for all our efforts. It was not as if there were any particular design in the opposition to our interest in rapeseed. In the simplest possible terms, it looked more like sheer inertia.

There were several government departments we thought ought to be concerned about the future of rapeseed. The Department of Agriculture was an obvious candidate. But we also felt the Department of Trade and Commerce with their responsibility for overseas sales markets should be developing the foreign market for rapeseed. We thought their trade counselors ought to be out looking for countries to use our rapeseed, locating the foreign crushing mills for the seed. They were not doing any of that.

We assumed, correctly, as it turned out, that if there were any opposition at all to the development of rapeseed as a major agricultural product in Canada, it would probably come from the Department of Transport, although for the life of me I could not figure out why Transport did not want to help these farmers. For years the railway companies had opposed hauling grain at existing rates. They had all opposed adding rapeseed to the list of approved grains under the Railway Act. There were still senior department officials in Transport who accepted the view that rapeseed just did not really qualify under the Railway Act because it was not that sort of grain.

There is often a rather cozy old-boy relationship between senior officials in certain branches of government and the particular industry the department is presumed to regulate, and it was true in Transport. The railway companies and the department often ran along parallel tracks with the same destination in mind. I did not know that then. Back in those early days I was very much a novice in the weird and mysterious workings of the government machine.

One day, I was talking to an understanding, mid-level official of the department. I asked him why in heaven's name we could not get a fair hearing on the rapeseed deal from his department? His reply was remarkable both for its candor and for its sympathy.

"In my experience, government acts at pressure point. There are just not any I can spot for you at the present time. Indifference is by far the worst enemy of progress and improvement. Particularly so if it originates from outside the established circles."

I must have looked shocked because he went on to say: "Once a scheme comes sailing out of senior management, it goes right to the top and has a more-than-even chance to be put into action. There is another obstacle you have right now. Your party has a comparatively new government with untried ministers. The gears just are not meshing between the ministry and the top officials. Unless there is a clear directive from the top—that is, from the Prime Minister's office—no official is going to go out on a limb on an issue like rapeseed."

How very right he was.

The bureaucrats generally had no time for us. We could not get to see official records. When we talked about lower freight rates under the Crow's Nest Pass rates, and research for wider commercial usage of rapeseed, we were given the brush-off. In truth the issue was regarded, I think, as being just a little bit silly. Maybe it was the name, "rapeseed." It is called "canola" these days.

By the late 1950s annual production had dwindled to a pitifully small amount. Then we discovered a "pressure point." It started with a trip I made to the north from Ottawa on constituency business. I met E. Bogosch, a businessman with extensive farm holdings in the Peace River area. He grew a lot of rapeseed on those farms. He was also a major exporter of rapeseed. Bogosch told me he was having a real scrap with the railway over the freight rates. He had just shipped some carload lots of the seed to Vancouver by CNR, and it was all earmarked for export. Although he was curious about how I was doing in Ottawa on my end of the fight over rapeseed, he questioned whether it would be of any help to him. I admitted we were not making much headway. But as we talked, it came to me that his case might bring this whole thing out into the open. There he was, wanting the CNR to give him a special rate, a rate for grain;

and there they were, rejecting his request on the ground that rapeseed was not a grain. Bogosch was a tough customer. If he stayed firm, the matter had to end up in a legal battle over the nature of rapeseed. We talked about it and promised to stay in touch.

A little while later after my return to Ottawa, Bogosch telephoned me. The CNR had seized his grain. They would release it only upon payment in full of the freight charges they were demanding. He was refusing to pay. No doubt the next step would be their taking further steps to dispose of his rapeseed to cover their claim. The time for a proper response had arrived.

Bogosch came to Ottawa. We decided it would be best to take the dispute to the Board of Transport commissioners because, as I told Bogosch, it would provide a simpler and cleaner way to get the issue out for public consideration. We would ask the Transport board to declare rapeseed a grain within the meaning of the Railway Act. Going into a court of law for a decision could be lengthy; it would be expensive. I felt the Transport board had more leeway to consider the economic and technical aspects of the dispute. Bogosch agreed and instructed me to proceed as counsel.

I made a search for precedents, and I canvassed some of my friends who were experienced in the continuous freight-rate hearings among the railway companies and the western provinces, and certain farm organizations. The proceedings were filed, the CNR replied, and the case was duly set for a hearing before a panel of the Board of Transport commissioners. We had an arguable, although not necessarily a powerful, proposition to make that rapeseed qualified for the lower grain freight rate. We intended to introduce evidence about rapeseed, its qualities, and the efficient methods by which it was grown. We further decided we might do better if we obtained most of our evidence from an unusual group. We would ask the western Members of Parliament, who were also practical farmers and who had experience of growing rapeseed, to testify as expert witnesses. They agreed. We found them quite happy to do so.

Because this was, in part, something of a public relations exercise, we gathered everybody together for a photo session on the steps of Centre Block on Parliament Hill. We were all there: my fellow Members of Parliament, now soon-to-be-called-on "expert witnesses"; Eldon Williams, the assistant counsel; and Alvin Hamilton, the cabinet minister from Saskatchewan. After the press took its pictures, we filed over to the old Union Station, opposite the Chateau Laurier. That was where the Transport Board held its sittings in Ottawa. Bogosch was due to arrive later so we started without him.

Sitting at the counsel table opposite us was an imposing array of senior railway legal talent, buttressed by their vice-presidents, and a number of other officials. Several government civil servants were hovering anxiously on the sidelines. On our side we also had the benefit of the talent of Jim Frawley, the Alberta government's legal representative in Ottawa, one of the brightest minds in the field of railway law and freight rates in the country.

The Members of Parliament were placed on the stand, and after being sworn, each testified to his farming experience, his knowledge of rapeseed, and his knowledge of growing it. In general, their evidence established that in all respects such as preparation of soil, seeding, combining, and so forth, rapeseed was not unlike any other grain to grow. We presented evidence about the nature of the seed itself and we told them the success story of its production during the war years, in case anyone had forgotten.

There was one humorous incident. Everytime our witness, Reynold Rapp, testified one of the commissioners kept calling him "Mr. Rape." I thought of that some years later when a post office in Saskatchewan, a centre of rapeseed farming, used for a short while a cancellation mark on its envelopes. It read the "Land of Rape and Honey."

The hearing lasted a day. At the end of the hearing, the Board of Transport commissioners chose to reserve judgment. This annoyed the railway people who had expected an immediate dismissal. After some weeks a decision was handed down with written reasons. The panel divided: the majority agreed to dismiss our application; but, a minority of two thought differently and came down in our favor. The CNR won the round, but it was a Pyrrhic victory because the minority decision was closely reasoned and written in such clear terms we could use it to press ahead with our campaign. And we did.

The hearing had been well covered in the press. We now

found that formerly recalcitrant government officials were much more responsive to our requests for information. This helped us sharpen our attacks in the House. That gave us even more media coverage, and we circulated copies of everything among our colleagues—the information we were getting from the government, the press reports, responses from our constituents, and the judgment itself. In short, we kept pushing at that one "pressure point."

It was not long before a number of farmers in the west began to campaign actively. A great many of John Diefenbaker's constituents from the Prince Albert district flooded him with petitions and letters. It was clear the logjam was breaking.

The first indication we had was when we were quietly told that George Hees, the Minister of Transport, would soon introduce a government bill to amend the Railway Act. By statute rapeseed would be declared a "grain" for the purpose of receiving the reduced freight rates for export. Then we learned the government was interested in proceeding with experiments to improve the seed. They wanted to find a seed even more compatible with our soil and climate, and to reduce the erucic acid content which made the product less suitable for human consumption as a vegetable oil. There was yet another blessing. Instructions were sent to government trade officials overseas to explore the world for potential markets. It was not hard to find them. There were cities in Europe and Asia with a demand for the grain and the crushing mills to handle it.

Reynold Rapp and I worked closely to keep up the pressure. He was in his own quiet, persevering way a most effective member. Looking back, I can recall his maiden speech. He told the House that when he first came to Ottawa, he went up to Parliament Hill, walked around a bit, looked at the statues of the great Canadians there—John A. Macdonald, Wilfrid Laurier, Robert Borden—and thought how wonderful it was that the country had received him too, an immigrant boy, who was now going to sit in the same place as these earlier Canadians. It was an impressive speech. Rapp later became the chief government whip.

As history reveals, rapeseed acquired new respectability as a crop, the seed was improved, byproducts appeared, and a good market for the oil was established worldwide. At about the time we started the struggle to reinstate its value to the nation, we were producing little more than 200,000 bushels at a price of slightly over $2.00/bushel. Several years later, after the fight was won, we produced in one year alone 100 million bushels at $9.00/bushel. Had the future of rapeseed been left to the oversight and neglect of the Ottawa bureaucrats, it would never have become the important cash crop it is today for the farmers of northwestern Canada.

CHAPTER THIRTEEN

The Peter Treu Case

THE PETER TREU CASE IS A CLASSIC EXAMPLE OF WHAT can be done to an individual who just will not lie down and play good dog when government officials and agencies snap their fingers.

Treu came to this country from West Germany, in due course becoming a citizen and settling with his family in Montreal's Beaconsfield suburb. He was a brilliant engineer specializing in communications. Treu had worked for a number of NATO countries and their armed forces, and was now carrying on the same work in Canada in the 1970s with Northern Electric, a Canadian company under contract to NADGECO. NADGECO was the NATO entity with responsibility for supply and procurement. The nature of Treu's work, which involved attending many closed meetings in Canada and abroad, required him to have security clearance. Throughout his many years of service, not only in Canada, but in various NATO countries, there had never been any complaint, charge, or suggestion of irregularities. Then one day he found himself secretly charged under Canada's Official Secrets Act.

Like other Canadians, I had read several stories in the press about the secret trial of the Montreal engineer under the Official Secrets Act, and had noted questions asked in the House of Commons by some members, including Otto Jelinek, the Halton Progressive Conservative MP. On orders of the day, Jelinek, obviously supplied with some information, asked government ministers if Dr. Treu's prosecution was linked in any way to espionage or the sale of secrets to mainland China. The answer was a categorical "no."

Significantly, this exchange coincided with an important aspect of the prosecution's case, which developed the next day. It surely looked like there had to be some relationship. Treu's counsel were furious at the unsubstantiated implications of the House questioning. They wrote an angry letter to the justice minister. However, once questions are asked in Parliament, the matter comes into the public domain. It is quite impossible to remove the stigma. Any denial contained in a ministerial reply is rarely taken into account. Subsequently, the appeal court referred to in its judgment what the Crown had attempted to smuggle into the case as an irrelevant issue about China. But how ironic. Here were authorities prosecuting for breach of information security, who had absolutely no hesitation about arranging to make public exceedingly sensitive material, material which, if true, would certainly be covered by the Official Secrets Act.

There is a further point to consider. Had there been any substance to the innuendo, can there be any doubt that the government would have discovered it already and laid charges accordingly? It was a red herring, an attempt by the Crown to bolster a weak case and make Treu look like a traitor.

Those in government with a special axe to grind or a special plea often use the ploy of arranging that certain data go to a member who, quite properly, will bring the matter to the attention of the government in the House by seeking information during question period. My resentment is against high-ranking government authorities who rant about the dangers that could result from more openness in parliamentary democracy, yet have not the slightest hesitation in employing the ancient and dishonorable system of deliberately leaking information for their own purposes.

I filed away these meagre bits of information, having by then concluded that the Official Secrets Act in its existing form was not only bad legislation, but a formidable obstacle to the opening-up of government information as well. The two were simply incompatible. Under the act, which provides for the holding of secret trials, it is essential to have all sentences passed in open court. I still knew very little about the facts of the case. But as a lawyer and parliamentarian, I thought the whole thing left a bad taste—that a court could go underground like a badger, surfacing only briefly to pass sentence, with nobody, other than the actual participants, knowing what was going on. The true spirit of any trial is that proceedings are held in the presence of the public, and the examination of witnesses takes place in open court. While some miscarriages of justice do occur, this practice provides a more likely prospect of getting at the truth and ensuring justice is done.

My next intelligence came from news reports that a two-year sentence had been imposed on Dr. Alexander Peter Treu. Leaving the courthouse, Dr. Treu was met by reporters. He answered a few questions, all harmless replies which in no way reflected on the court, but the judge called him back to the bench and cautioned him sternly. He was ordered not to discuss the case with anyone except his lawyers—this, despite the fact the case had been concluded in the trial court. Treu had been convicted and sentenced. But the harassment did not end there. An application for bail pending appeal was granted on the specific condition he remain silent about the case; this was at the demand of counsel for the Crown. If this condition were broken, Treu was to be taken into custody and held in jail pending hearing of his appeal.

A few days after Treu's conviction and sentencing, I had a visit from a Montreal couple, friends and neighbors of the Treus. They slipped into my office as inconspicuously as they could. Nervously they admitted they feared the security people would seize them if it were suspected they were discussing the case with a Member of Parliament. The climate of secrecy, the cloak-and-dagger atmosphere, the warning from the court had alarmed them. They feared they might have been followed to my office. They feared their telephone was bugged. It was altogether a very sad state of affairs in a so-called democratic country. As friends of Treu, the couple wanted to know if anything could be done to help him. Would he be permanently muzzled, forbidden to talk about his case, trial, and sentence? Could I, or anyone, find out what the government and security forces were up to? Would I help?

"I'll do what I can," I assured them, "but I'll have to see and talk to him, find out firsthand the facts, and get the complete background picture."

"But what about the gag rule? Can they make it stick, stop him from talking to you?"

"Yes, it would apply to us both. We'll cross that bridge when we come to it. Tell me, how do I get in touch with him?"

After warning me they were certain at least one of his phones was tapped, they suggested a number to call. In due course I reached Treu and arranged a meeting, but before we could come together, there was another interesting development.

Earlier I had asked some questions in the House of the Prime Minister and some of the department ministers involved in the case. I wanted information about the secrecy of the trial and about the gag placed on Treu after his sentence. I also wanted to know why the hearing was held before a comparatively new occupant of a provincial court bench when, in the past, most trials under the Act had been launched in the supreme court. Although I had tried not to use language that could be construed as a criticism of the trial judge, there had been an immediate and indignant reaction from the Montreal court. Listening to the radio one morning, I heard my name mentioned. The chief judge of the provincial court was quoted as saying, "Mr. Baldwin was out of line and had no business intervening. He should restrict himself to his role as a Member of Parliament and leave this and other cases to the courts and judges."

The statement seemed to me a thinly veiled threat and a wrongful attack on the independence of Members of Parliament. I had been a member of the bar for fifty years and I certainly respected the independence of the judiciary. But, they are no more free from reasonable and objective criticism than myself or, for that matter, the Prime Minister of the country. Moreover, my statements were made in the House and therefore subject to parliamentary immunity. I thought I had not just a right, but a plain duty to take issue with the conduct of a trial that appeared to reach beyond the bounds of proper judicial conduct, a trial which looked like a breach of natural justice and human rights. The courts should not be placed beyond the scope of reasonable discussion and criticism any more than other social groups. This was a challenge not to be ignored; I hurried to my parliamentary office in the Confederation Building to examine precedents, a copy of the news report, and to decide on appropriate action.

Later that day I rose in the Commons on a question of parliamentary privilege, based on the clear and certain principle that my rights and duties as a Member of Parliament to function without threat or challenge were jeopardized by the statements of the chief judge, aimed at limiting my freedom of action in the Treu case. I requested the usual remedies and, as required by the Standing Orders of the Day, sent a notice to Mr. Speaker so the matter would have priority after 3:00 p.m. that day. The outcome was a spirited debate on the entire question.

Many members took part, including Stanfield, Diefenbaker, and Clark.

For the first time the Treu case, which the authorities had been contriving to sweep under the rug, was exposed in all its sordidness to Parliament, the press, and the public. The debate provided an excellent opportunity to put on record some of the extraordinary facts which had come into my possession. In my argument I suggested the judge, who had made threats against me, be called before the bar of the House of Commons to explain and justify his actions. The next day the judge left Montreal, saying he was going for a holiday in Greece. A few days later, the Speaker, after expressing some doubts, ruled against my motion. Nevertheless, it had been a useful exercise and there was no way now that the security agencies could "put the toothpaste back into the tube."

Governments, at least those élite at the top levels, both elected and appointed, are like the Bourbons. They never learn. They are human (despite views expressed to the contrary), and subject to miscalculations, misconceptions, and an occasional misdemeanor. This does not always bother them as far as the public is concerned. Nevertheless, governments are desperate to present a facade of infallibility. When something is not as it ought to be, it is corraled and thrown in the Augean stables. In some cases there are leaks and mistakes, which once exposed, become magnified out of all proportion to their original significance.

Peter Treu and I eventually met in my office following several telephone discussions. He was a tall, well-built, good-looking man in his mid-fifties, intelligent and articulate. Obviously, too, he was a person impatient with stupidity, and not one to suffer fools easily. The sort of person who is very likely to tangle with any bureaucracy.

I entered into an arrangement with Treu which permitted him to speak to me without his liberty being threatened. He would consider me one of his counsel. Although I was not admitted to practice at the Quebec bar, this did not prevent me from advising him. Further, since he would pay me no fee, I could also speak freely in the House without being charged with a conflict of interest.

Treu told me his work with the NATO countries had been in the development and improvement of a highly successful communications system. After arriving in Canada he continued with the project as an employee of Northern Electric. They had the Canadian contract for a portion of the overall concept. Because some NATO programs had commercial as well as military significance, it was a practice to share between the member countries various development and manufacturing phases. Security checks were run on all personnel engaged in this work. This had been done on Treu and was a continuation of the security clearance he had been given during his many years in West Germany.

Treu said that for corporate reasons, Northern Electric had decided to withdraw from the NATO contract, and had invited him to become the prime Canadian contractor, a definite sign of their confidence in him. In addition, a number of sectors of the Canadian government involved in the project urged him to take on the work as prime contractor. After considering the options, he agreed. He formed his own company and renewed the various arrangements with NADGECO.

At the time, Treu did much of his work from his Beaconsfield home where he kept a great many of the records he required. These were kept under secure arrangements which had never been challenged by his employer or security authorities in the past. The Canadian government did have a set of applicable security regulations, detailed, lengthy, and unknown to most of the people working covered by them. Perhaps they were available only to the security professionals who lived and worked in a queer twilight zone of their own. Treu had never been informed that the regulations included a provision that in all cases when an employee changed employers, it was necessary to apply for and obtain a completely new security clearance. Common sense would dictate that if this rule were applicable to Treu's case, there would be an immediate, automatic compliance when he set up to work as the head of his own company to do the same sort of work he had been doing as the employee of another.

When I asked how he had learned of the requirement, he replied, "I didn't know a thing until some time after I had carried on with the new set-up. I happened to run into an old friend who had been a security official of my former employer. He told me the score."

"And what did you do then?"

"I hustled back to my office and made an application to have the required transfer made."

"Did anyone say anything to you?"

"No, nothing. So I figured everything was all right."

He added he was a trained professional, engaged in a highly complicated and important job. He never gave another thought to the question of security clearance. He simply continued with his work and even received additional contracts.

What a shock it was to him then when, without warning, members of the RCMP security force descended upon his home one day and carried away several hundred pounds of documents.

Angry and baffled, he went to the Department of Supply and Services with which he was closely associated, as well as to other agencies and departments, looking for answers. Why were his documents seized? And how was he to work without essential records? No one could or would tell him anything. It was not until several years later that he heard a Supply and Services department security official testify that Treu's security had been cancelled *without notice to him,* and that no new clearance had been issued upon his application, again, *without informing him!* That was why Treu was in breach of the regulations.

What a travesty!

It seemed to me a gross violation of every principle of decency and rational conduct—to withdraw Treu's security clearance, deny the new application, not tell him, yet allow him to work for many months on security-rated jobs. Even more peculiar was that after the raid and seizure, he continued with his work. He still attended classified meetings. He still received additional contracts.

I subsequently learned that the authorities kept the material they seized, while conducting an exhaustive series of investigations, checks, and individual examinations over a period of two years in Canada and other parts of the world. Such activities are costly. I have been told that expenses for the investigation escalated into several hundreds of thousands of dollars. I was unable to check the accuracy of this report because security operations and their costs are well-concealed. I can think of nothing that more clearly illustrates the danger of unaccountable governmental handling of security. Once an investigation reaches a certain level, it simply acquires a life of its own. And most certainly, once spending of this magnitude occurs, those involved feel a responsibility to justify their work and costs. That often means the laying of charges. Someone has to be the victim. Decent people may well recoil from the assumption, but it has happened. Not just in other so-called democratic societies, but in Canada as well. For wrongdoing to triumph, it is only necessary for people of integrity to remain silent.

What happened next in the strange case of Dr. Peter Treu? Surely, if there had been subversion, or espionage, or actionable disloyalty, or the sale of military or other secrets, or any real threat to the country, it would have been discovered. Charges would have been laid accordingly.

All that was produced after the mountain moved, and shook, and rumbled for such a long time were two little mice: one, a charge that Treu was in possession of classified papers (his own), without having a proper security system (even though he had been using the same system for many years); two, a charge that Treu was in possession of classified papers (his own), without having a security clearance (which had been clandestinely taken away from him).

How did these ridiculous charges come to be laid? On whose authority? On whose advice? What documents were produced to persuade the attorney general of Canada that the safety and security of the realm depended upon the prosecution and conviction of this man on such silly and trumped-up allegations?

In the fall of 1978 I travelled to Montreal for Treu's appeal. It was held before three judges of the Quebec Court of Appeal. I was not able to participate in the argument because I was not a member of the Quebec bar, although I had discussions with Treu's two counsel and sat in on the hearing.

His lawyers conducted a magnificent plea, very skillfully putting forward every possible argument. The decision, which was reserved, came out early in 1979. The three judges were unanimous in allowing the appeal and setting aside the conviction and sentence. The final stage of the prosecution, or persecution, of Dr. Peter Treu under the Official Secrets Act had produced a legal victory for Treu.

I considered the substance of the judgment to be a strong indictment of the government and department authorities involved and, in general, a useful addition to the jurisprudence concerned with such a dangerous piece of legislation as the Official Secrets Act. Wisely, the government decided to let the matter rest and not go on to the Supreme Court of Canada.

An attempt was made to persuade authorities to compensate Treu for the injustice perpetrated against him, but they remained stubbornly intolerant and refused.

Eventually, Dr. Treu went through a marriage break-up. An embittered and tragic figure, he left Canada. He had lost his property, his family, his professional career, and his faith in this country and its laws. However, since I first wrote this chapter, I learned Peter Treu has returned to Canada. He is attempting to rehabilitate his career and start again in Toronto. I had a chance to see him recently, and I feel he is doing his best to put his difficult experiences behind him.

Afterword

If these stories give some insight into the character of the inhabitants of the north, some of the tales are also confirmation of the way authority manhandles facts and rules just to have its way. Truth is essential for the proper functioning of the courts. It is also required in the conduct of the business of the public and certainly in our legislatures. After all, Parliament has been called the highest Court in the land.

From time to time conditions in Parliament and government occasionally allowed those with a good case, with ample public support to upset that ritual bureaucratic minuet, to challenge bad decisions by getting at the facts. It does not happen often enough and actually it is getting harder and harder to do so. In Parliament the tentacles of the octopus party system have tightened their grip. Officialdom fibs, fudges, and fiddles. It is most difficult for private Members of Parliament to follow as individuals the creative and productive role many of them desire. This is a distemper of our parliamentary system.

The recent case in the U.K of the attempt by Margaret Thatcher to seal off the publication of the book by former spycatcher Peter Wright describing the fantastic operations of the British Intelligence agency shows what people will do to suppress the facts. And then there is the Iran arms sale and diversion soap opera in Washinton.

When the Peter Treu case was running its course in Ottawa there was an indirect warning to me through a senior member of the Press Gallery via two of my colleagues that I would be wise to lay off my public interest in the issue.

I would sit in the House and sometimes wonder how much progress we had made over the last 400 years or so, since Catherine Drinker Bowen in her very readable book *The Lion and the Throne* described the English Parliament.

The House of Commons chamber is called small and crowded with four tiers of benches rising on three sides, leaving not nearly enough room for everyone to sit. When a vote division was called, she writes, "The Ayes walked out the lobby door, losing their seats to those who were standing. Weaker souls who cared more for comfort than principle promptly voted No so as to retain their seats." Who knows? This may be as shrewd a reason for casting a vote as being told to do so by the Whip.

I have known in the past, and still do, so many bright, articulate, and conscientious men and women who are elected and come to Ottawa anxious to do the right thing. What do they find? Too often they discover they just cannot penetrate the swamps and mazes which protect institutionalized government.

I leave off here with the hope that the characteristics of strength, independence, and challenge which brought people to the north and marked their progress will yet come to the legislatures of our country, so that they will, in a variation of the charge to a jury in a criminal trial, "make true deliverance between the people and the government."

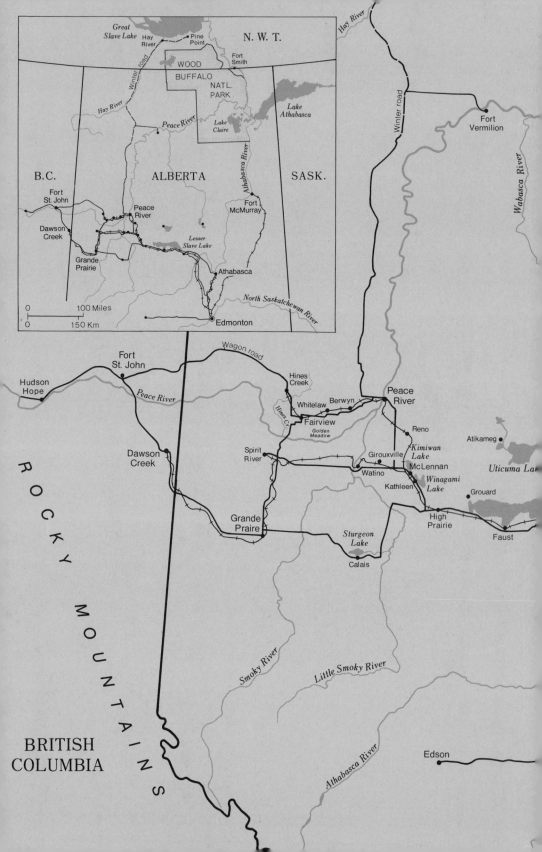